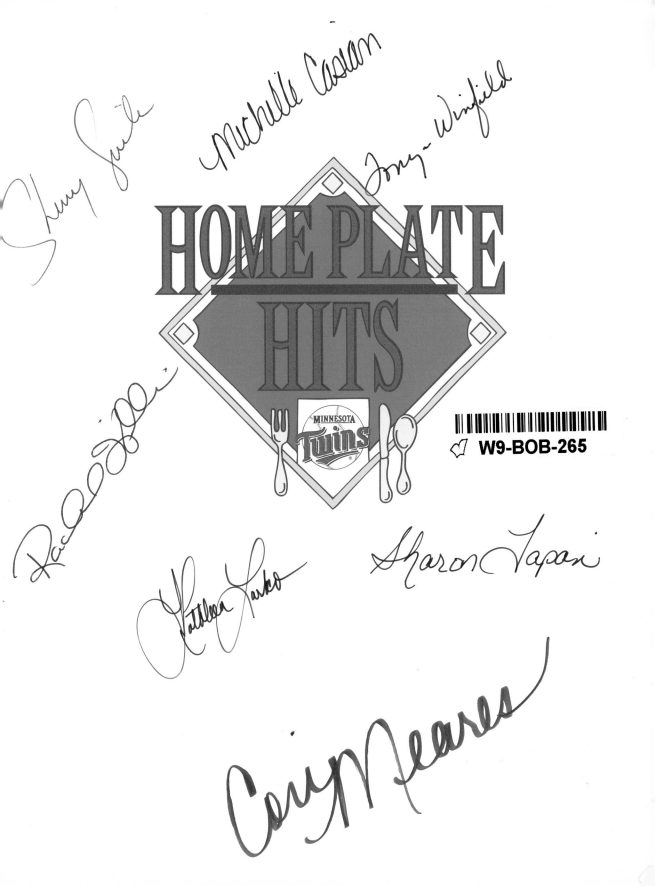

W9-BOB-265

Recipes from the Kitchens of the Minnesota Twins' Wives, Players, and Staff

Waldman House Press • Minneapolis

Thanks from the Minnesota Twins' wives to Kelly Services.

Order additional copies from the publisher. Try your bookstore first.
Cover price plus $3.50 for postage and handling.

Waldman House Press, Inc. 525 North Third Street, Minneapolis, MN 55401

Design and production by MacLean & Tuminelly

Illustrations by Caroline Price

Printed on 100-pound Mountie Matte from Potlatch Company, Cloquet, Minnesota

ISBN 0-931674-27-1   First Printing

 # Introduction

When I was asked to hit leadoff by writing the introduction to this book, I was quite surprised, flattered and honored. Although I come from a city renowned for its food, New Orleans, and from a family with a long line of chefs, I was still somewhat hesitant. But I saw this as so much more than a cookbook.

As the wives and significant others of professional baseball players, we often find ourselves carrying the majority of the load when caring for our families. Because of our husbands' unusual schedules, our responsibilities include everything from taking care of the children and home to organizing travel schedules, managing finances, pursuing our own careers and interests and, as always, supporting our husbands' careers.

Professional athletes have a high profile in the community and are often asked to participate in charitable events. Many times we are asked to participate with them— or sometimes requests will come in asking specifically for our involvement alone. The dilemma was finding the time to do all we would like to and still have the most significant impact on the charitable causes most meaningful to us.

After a great deal of thought, we decided to do one major project that could raise a significant amount of money and benefit multiple causes. We wanted to pursue a fun project, one in which we could show our creative sides. Hence, *Home Plate Hits* was born.

As the book progressed, excitement grew and everyone got involved. We received some wonderful recipes from our confirmed bachelors (including the phone numbers to several take-outs which we didn't include). Carl and Eloise Pohlad joined us, then coaches, the Twins front office and even the Twins' private chef.

The result is one of the most eclectic collections of recipes anywhere. They come from all across the country and from many walks of life. Some are the favorite pre-game meals of the players; others developed out of players' superstitions and the rest are long-time family favorites. We spiced our cookbook with lots of anecdotes, and seasoned the contents by providing some inside scoops on the players and their families. You will find photos of private moments, early days in the players' lives, and a photo gallery from some famous kitchens—you may cook and laugh at the same time!

And finally we have so many people to thank for helping us make this dream a reality. First and foremost our hats off to Ned and Brett Waldman at Waldman House Press for their confidence, guidance, and great vision. Also at Waldman House, we thank Dimitria Thorson for coordinating and helping in the selection of our many recipes, and Dan Verdick, whose passion for baseball gives our book a Twins fan's flavor.

Thanks to the Minnesota Twins Staff and General Counsel for making sure we crossed our t's and dotted our i's, and for their help in directing the funds to the projects we choose. To all the people who contributed recipes to this book—we bugged you endlessly but you were always so gracious. Because of the nature of baseball, some families and players who contributed are no longer with the team. We hope we've added to the good memories they have given Twins fans over the years.

Kudos to Andy King, our photographer, who worked so well with our fleeting schedules and satisfied all of us with his photographic genius and creativity.

Finally, lest we forget our husbands and family members who put up with the meetings, late-night phone calls, endless taste-testing, frayed nerves and the like. We couldn't have done it without you.

We sincerely hope you enjoy *Home Plate Hits*. These recipes were given with a lot of love and with the hope that you will enjoy them and the time you share with others around the table. We know at least one of them will prove to be a hit or a home run. And if cooking isn't your forte, you can order dinner in and still have fun thumbing through the photos and reading about your favorite Twins and their families.

Bon Appetit!

Tonya Winfield

Tonya Winfield

Table of Contents

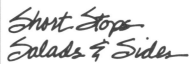

Short Stops
Salads & Sides

Sweet Spot Desserts

WHO'S WHO

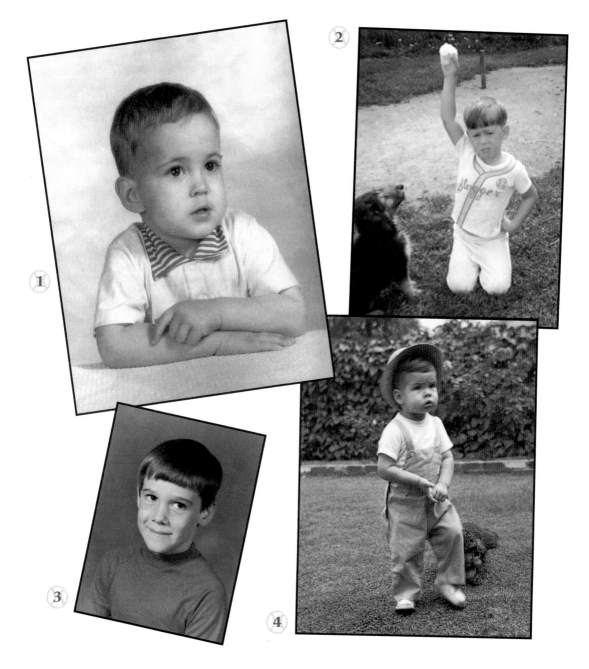

Warm-Ups

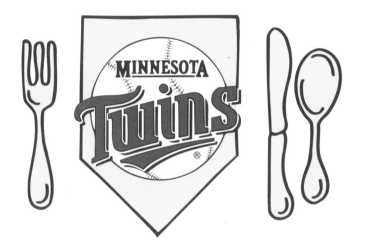

Warm-Ups

Opening Day Apple Dip
4

Ace Artichoke Dip
5

Stuffed Artichoke Hearts
6

Kaat's Broccoli Dip
7

Cheese Cookies
8

Triple Cheese Dip
9

Big League
Baked Chicken Wings
10

Double Cheese Ball
11

Dozen Deviled Eggs
12

Deviled Chicken
13

Pot o' Chili Dip
14

Great Grab Clam Dip
15

Cocktail Meatballs
16

Crack of the Bat
Crackers and Crab
17

Stuffed Mushrooms
Italian Style
18

Girl-Boy Dill Dip
19

Southpaw Shrimp Dip
20

Pitcher's Postgame Pizza
21

Taco Dip
22

Good Catch Vegetable Dip
23

Spinach Squares
24

Bourbon Hot Dogs
25

Opening Day Apple Dip

from Chris and Brian Harper

Awesome dip! Good with banana slices too. To keep fresh fruit from browning, squeeze lemon juice over fruit slices and toss to coat.

❝ Great for any occasion, from snacking kids to New Year's Eve parties. It's always a hit! ❞

—Chris Harper

LINE UP

8 ounces cream cheese, softened
¾ cup brown sugar
¼ cup sugar

1 teaspoon vanilla
sliced Granny Smith apples

PLAY-BY-PLAY

1. Blend all ingredients except apples until smooth.
2. Spoon into serving dish and serve with apple slices.

Serves 8

Unless otherwise directed in recipe, measure brown sugar by packing into the appropriate dry measuring cup and pressing firmly with a spoon until level.

Ace Artichoke Dip

from Sherry and Rick Aguilera

LINE UP

1 cup mayonnaise
8 ounces cream cheese
1 cup shredded Monterey Jack
   cheese
½ cup grated parmesan cheese
¼ teaspoon garlic salt

2 6-ounce jars marinated
   artichoke hearts, drained
   and diced
1 tablespoon chopped parsley
12-14 slices wheat bread,
   toasted and cut in fourths

PLAY-BY-PLAY

1. In small saucepan, combine mayonnaise, cheeses, and garlic salt. Cook and stir over low heat until cheeses melt. Stir in artichokes.

2. Add chopped parsley. Remove from heat and arrange on serving dish with toast points. Have a knife handy for spreading.

Serves 8-10

❝ I made this appetizer the first Christmas Rick and I were together, 1985. His family loved it! ❞

—Sherry Aguilera

Stuffed Artichoke Hearts

from Lori and Jim Deshaies

" Me, the old lady, a couple of Harleys and the open road. "

—Jim Deshaies' ultimate vacation

LINE UP

3 14-ounce cans artichoke hearts
8 ounces cream cheese, softened
¼ cup finely chopped green onion
¼ teaspoon garlic salt

⅛ teaspoon pepper
¼ cup butter, melted
½ cup freshly grated parmesan cheese

PLAY-BY-PLAY

1. Preheat oven to 400 degrees.

2. Squeeze artichoke hearts gently to drain. If necessary, thinly slice off bottom so hearts stand upright. Separate leaves to hollow out middle.

3. Combine cream cheese, onion, garlic salt and pepper. Mound mixture into hearts. Roll hearts in melted butter and then in parmesan cheese.

4. Stand stuffed hearts in baking dish. Bake for 15 minutes until hot and bubbly.

Serves 8-10

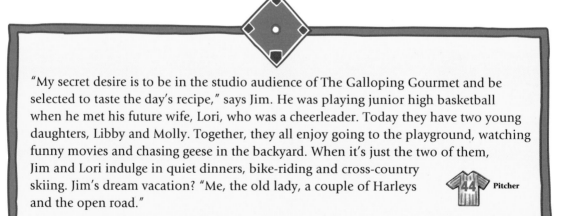

"My secret desire is to be in the studio audience of The Galloping Gourmet and be selected to taste the day's recipe," says Jim. He was playing junior high basketball when he met his future wife, Lori, who was a cheerleader. Today they have two young daughters, Libby and Molly. Together, they all enjoy going to the playground, watching funny movies and chasing geese in the backyard. When it's just the two of them, Jim and Lori indulge in quiet dinners, bike-riding and cross-country skiing. Jim's dream vacation? "Me, the old lady, a couple of Harleys and the open road."

44 Pitcher

Kaat's Broccoli Dip

from Mary Ann and Jim Kaat

Jim says his all-time favorite colors are "sky blue" and "grass green." He's seen a lot of both in his career in baseball, first as a player and then as a television announcer covering the Twins games.

LINE UP

8 ounces Velveeta cheese, cubed
1 can cream of mushroom soup
1 teaspoon garlic powder

10 ounces frozen chopped
broccoli, thawed
large-sized corn chips

PLAY-BY-PLAY

1. Melt Velveeta cheese in microwave, stirring often.

2. Add soup, garlic and broccoli to cheese, mix well. Serve warm with chips.

Serves 12

> ❝ An old family favorite—fast and easy and always gets raves. ❞
>
> —Jim Kaat

 Dip will keep in refrigerator for five days. Just reheat in the microwave and enjoy.

Cheese Cookies

from Rachel and Carl Willis

LINE UP

1 cup butter, softened
8 ounces sharp cheddar cheese,
grated
2½ cups sifted flour

1 teaspoon salt
½ teaspoon cayenne pepper
1 cup chopped pecans

PLAY-BY-PLAY

1. Cream butter until light. Add cheese and continue creaming until fluffy.

2. Sift together flour, salt and cayenne. Gradually add to butter-cheese mixture. Knead until dough is soft enough to shape.

3. Divide dough into fourths. Shape each fourth into a roll with 1¼-inch diameter. Wrap individual rolls in waxed paper. Chill overnight, at least 12 hours.

4. Preheat oven to 325 degrees. Lightly grease baking sheets. Slice each chilled roll into 15 cookies, arrange on sheets and bake for 10-12 minutes.

Makes 5 dozen cookies

"We have so little time together that when we do, we like to do things as a family," Carl says, speaking of his wife Rachel and children Alexandria Blake and Daniel Shelton. This includes taking the kids on outings, going to movies or eating out. The sporting life doesn't let up in the off-season, when Carl golfs and "watches any kind of sport." Carl's secret wish is to sing with Earth, Wind and Fire.

51 Pitcher

Triple Cheese Dip

from Andrea and Mark Guthrie

The Guthries love the outdoors, walking the beach, jet-skiing, jogging and golf. When it's time to pitch in and cook, they like their recipes simple and delicious, just like this winning combination. Indoors or out, you'll have the crowd cheering for more.

❝ This dip is extremely easy to make and it is very good, yet not good for the dieter! ❞

—Andrea Guthrie

LINE UP

1 cup shredded cheddar cheese
1 cup shredded Monterey Jack cheese

1 cup shredded Swiss or Colby cheese
1 cup mayonnaise
1 small Vidalia onion, chopped

PLAY-BY-PLAY

1. Preheat oven to 300 degrees.

2. Combine all ingredients, mixture will be clumpy. Transfer to 2-quart baking dish.

3. Bake for 20 minutes, until melted. Serve hot with chips or crackers.

Serves 12

Pedro "Petey" Muñoz played baseball, basketball and volleyball for Dr. Pila High School in his home town of Ponce, Puerto Rico. It was his baseball talent that attracted the major leagues, and Pedro signed with the Toronto Blue Jays when he was only 16 years old. In 1990, he was traded to the Twins and made his major league debut later that year.

5 Outfield

Big League Baked Chicken Wings

from Pedro Muñoz

LINE UP

20-24 chicken wings
3 tablespoons butter

1 tablespoon plus 1½ teaspoons soy sauce
garlic salt and pepper to taste

PLAY-BY-PLAY

1. Preheat oven to 400 degrees. Rinse chicken and pat dry. Fold wing tips back so each wing forms a triangle.

2. Melt butter over low heat, stir in soy sauce and remove from heat. Dip chicken wings in sauce, then arrange on baking sheet. Sprinkle wings with garlic salt and pepper to taste.

3. Bake for 1 hour. Wings will be very crispy.

Serves 4-6

Carl, Alexandria, Daniel, and Rachel

Double Cheese Ball

from Rachel and Carl Willis

LINE UP

1 2½-ounce jar dried beef, chopped fine

1¾ pounds cream cheese, softened

3 tablespoons chopped onion

1 tablespoon dried chopped parsley

3 tablespoons Worcestershire sauce

2 dashes hot sauce

1 cup shredded cheddar cheese

2 tablespoons mayonnaise

¼ cup chopped green pepper

1 cup finely chopped pecans

PLAY-BY-PLAY

1. Thoroughly combine all ingredients except pecans.

2. Divide in half and form into two balls. Roll in pecans and refrigerate until firm. Serve with assorted crackers. Store in refrigerator.

Makes 2 large balls

> ❝ During the season, one of my main duties is to see that Lenny has a variety of cereal to eat. He has a certain cereal bowl (the 'Jethro' bowl) that he uses most of the time. When he's in a batting slump he changes bowls and says, 'there aren't any knocks in that bowl right now.' ❞
>
> —Robin Webster

Dozen Deviled Eggs

from Robin and Lenny Webster

Egg-ceptional deviled eggs. For a sure-fire way to hard-boil eggs, bring to a boil in a saucepan with a lid. Cover, then turn off heat. Let stand covered for 20 minutes. Rinse under cold water.

LINE UP

6 hard-boiled eggs
½ teaspoon mustard
3 tablespoons mayonnaise
¼ teaspoon salt

½ teaspoon vinegar
½ teaspoon Worcestershire sauce
dash pepper
paprika

PLAY-BY-PLAY

1. Halve eggs lengthwise and remove yolks to small mixing bowl.

2. Mash yolks with a fork and add rest of ingredients except paprika. Mix until fluffy.

3. Spoon mixture into egg whites and sprinkle with paprika. Arrange on serving platter and serve.

Serves 6

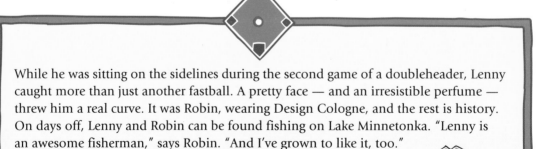

While he was sitting on the sidelines during the second game of a doubleheader, Lenny caught more than just another fastball. A pretty face — and an irresistible perfume — threw him a real curve. It was Robin, wearing Design Cologne, and the rest is history. On days off, Lenny and Robin can be found fishing on Lake Minnetonka. "Lenny is an awesome fisherman," says Robin. "And I've grown to like it, too." They love to travel and their favorite trip so far was honeymooning in Puerto Rico. Lenny's secret wish is to be an attorney.

15 Catcher

Deviled Chicken

from Rosemary and Brett Merriman

LINE UP

2 cups cooked shredded chicken
½ cup mayonnaise
3 tablespoons melted butter
2 tablespoons Dijon mustard
pinch cayenne pepper

1 cup fresh bread crumbs
¼ cup chopped fresh parsley
2 tablespoons butter, cubed fine
sliced French bread

Sports, food and fun all score big with Brett. If he weren't involved in baseball, he'd like to own a sports bar and grill.

PLAY-BY-PLAY

1. Preheat oven to 400 degrees.

2. Combine chicken, mayonnaise, melted butter, mustard and cayenne pepper. Spread into 9-inch pie plate.

3. Combine bread crumbs, parsley, and cubed butter. Sprinkle over chicken. Bake 25 minutes and serve warm with French bread.

Serves 6

Pot o' Chili Dip

from Cori and Pat Meares

> **ʕ** This dip was a Christmas gift to my family. Now this recipe has been adopted by us for a perfectly warm and delicious dip for the holidays. **ʖ**
>
> —Cori Meares

LINE UP

2 pounds ground beef
1 16-ounce roll of chili, sliced
2 onions, chopped fine
2 cloves garlic, minced
3 4½-ounce cans chopped
    green chiles

8 ounces picante sauce
1 teaspoon garlic salt
1 teaspoon chili powder
2 pounds Velveeta cheese
corn tortilla chips

PLAY-BY-PLAY

1. Brown ground beef and drain fat.

2. Combine all ingredients in crockpot set to low. Heat for 2 hours.

3. Serve warm with tortilla chips.

Serves 15

Great Grab Clam Dip

from Danielle and Derek Parks

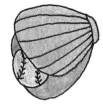

LINE UP

2 loaves sourdough bread, one round
1 6½-ounce can minced clams, drained

1 pound cream cheese, softened
2 tablespoons butter, melted
dash garlic salt

PLAY-BY-PLAY

1. Preheat oven to 225 degrees. Slice ½-inch off the top of the round sourdough loaf. Reserve top and scoop bread out of middle of loaf, keeping crust intact. Cube bread removed from the center as well as remaining loaf.

2. Combine clams, cream cheese, butter and garlic salt. Mound in hollowed loaf. Replace lid and wrap loaf in foil. Bake for 2 hours.

3. Remove from oven, unwrap and place on serving platter with cubed bread.

Serves 8

"Great catch, buddy!"

Wedding, 1987

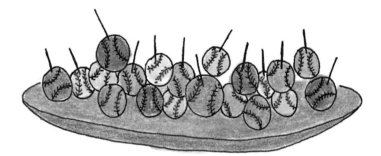

Cocktail Meatballs

from Marge and Jim Wiesner

Makes a great meat-loaf. Pat meat mixture into loaf and place in 9-by-5-inch loaf pan. Prepare half of chili-jelly sauce and pour over top. Bake for 1 hour.

LINE UP

1 pound ground beef
½ cup bread crumbs
1 small onion, minced
¼ cup milk
1 egg
1 tablespoon minced parsley

1 teaspoon salt
1 teaspoon pepper
½ teaspoon Worcestershire sauce
12 ounces chili sauce
10 ounces grape jelly

PLAY-BY-PLAY

1. Preheat oven to 325 degrees.

2. Combine beef, bread crumbs, onion, milk and egg. Add parsley, salt, pepper and Worcestershire sauce.

3. Gently shape meat into 1-inch balls. Arrange in broiler pan and bake for 15 minutes, turning once to cook evenly.

4. Heat chili sauce and jelly until melted together. Pour warm sauce over hot meatballs and stir until coated. Serve.

Makes 4 dozen meatballs

Crack of the Bat Crackers and Crab

from Lark and Andy MacPhail

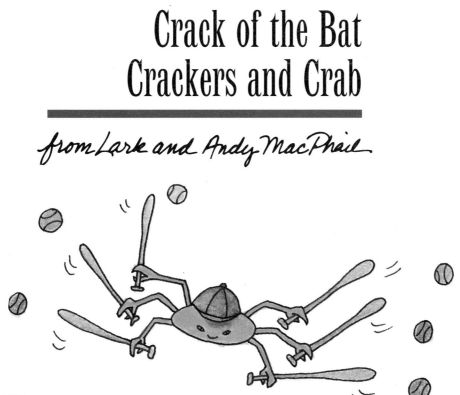

LINE UP

8 ounces cream cheese, softened
1 tablespoon milk or ⅓ cup
    mayonnaise
7 ounces crabmeat, fresh or
    drained if canned
2 tablespoons finely chopped
    onion

1 tablespoon horseradish
salt, pepper and tabasco sauce
    to taste
⅓ cup toasted almonds
assorted crackers

PLAY-BY-PLAY

1. Preheat oven to 375 degrees.

2. Combine cream cheese and milk or mayonnaise. Mix well. Add crab, onion, horseradish and seasonings to taste.

3. Spread mixture in ovenproof serving dish. Sprinkle with almonds and bake for 15 minutes. Serve warm with crackers.

Serves 8-10

Stuffed Mushrooms Italian Style

from Lisa Limbaugh and Eddie Guardado

❝ Eddie doesn't really have any one favorite food, but he does eat Cream of Wheat on the days he pitches. He will also tell you that he hates cheese – absolutely will not eat it. Yet two things he loves to eat are pizza and nachos. That's Eddie for you! ❞

—Lisa Limbaugh, Eddie Guardado's fiancée

Lisa's Dad is famous for making these at Christmas.

LINE UP

16 large fresh mushrooms, washed and stems chopped fine
6 ounces sweet Italian sausage
1 clove garlic, minced

3 tablespoons olive oil
2 tablespoons minced fresh parsley
¼ cup grated parmesan cheese
¼ cup water

PLAY-BY-PLAY

1. Preheat oven to 350 degrees.

2. Remove sausage from casing and place in sauté pan. Add chopped mushroom stems, garlic and 1 tablespoon of the olive oil. Cook, breaking up meat with fork until lightly browned.

3. Add 1 tablespoon olive oil, parsley and cheese to sausage. Fill mushroom caps, rounding off tops. Place stuffed mushrooms in shallow baking dish and add remaining tablespoon olive oil and water.

4. Bake mushrooms for 20 minutes. Serve hot.

Serves 8

Girl-Boy Dill Dip

from Cori and Pat Meares

❝ This is the popular 'Pat and Cori dip' that we always brought to 'girl-boy' parties while we were dating in junior high and high school. We continue to make this when entertaining guests or going to more 'girl-boy' parties. ❞

—Cori Meares

LINE UP

12 ounces sour cream
1½ cups mayonnaise
1 tablespoon dried diced onion
2 tablespoons dill weed

1 teaspoon garlic salt
1 teaspoon onion salt
1 teaspoon celery salt
chips and fresh vegetables

PLAY-BY-PLAY

1. Mix all ingredients and place in serving bowl.

2. Refrigerate at least 1 hour. Serve with chips and fresh vegetables.

Serves 6

Southpaw Shrimp Dip

from Lisa Limbaugh and Eddie Guardado

LINE UP

1 pound cream cheese, softened
1 cup mayonnaise
6 green onions, chopped

3 ribs celery, diced
½ pound cooked shrimp
crackers

PLAY-BY-PLAY

1. Combine cream cheese and mayonnaise, mix well.

2. Add onions, celery, and shrimp. Serve with crackers.

Serves 6-8

Pitcher's Postgame Pizza

from Sharon and Kevin Tapani

LINE UP

1 8-ounce can refrigerator
  crescent dinner rolls
8 ounces cream cheese, softened
⅓ cup mayonnaise
½ teaspoon onion salt
½ teaspoon dill weed

2 cups assorted vegetables such
  as carrots, cucumbers,
  broccoli, cauliflower and
  green pepper, cut small
½ cup shredded cheddar cheese
bacon bits

PLAY-BY-PLAY

1. Preheat oven to 400 degrees. Pinching seams together, spread rolls out on cookie sheet. Bake for 10 minutes, being careful not to overbake. Cool.

2. Combine cream cheese and mayonnaise until fluffy. Blend in onion salt and dill. Spread over crust. Top with vegetables and sprinkle with cheese and bacon bits.

3. Chill pizza well, at least 1 hour. Cut into serving pieces and arrange on serving platter.

Serves 6

Taco Dip

from Monica and David McCarty

❝ This recipe was adapted from our mothers' separate recipes. Great for get-togethers! ❞

—Monica McCarty

LINE UP

¾ pound ground beef, browned and drained

2 1¼-ounce packages taco seasoning mix

1 16-ounce can refried beans

salt and pepper to taste

4 ounces low fat sour cream

1 4¼-ounce can chopped black olives

2 4½-ounce cans chopped green chiles

4 tomatoes, chopped

1 purple onion, chopped

3 avocados, mashed

¾ pound each cheddar and Monterey Jack cheese, grated

corn tortilla chips

PLAY-BY-PLAY

1. Add one package of taco seasoning mix to ground beef and prepare as directed. In separate bowl, combine remaining package seasoning mix with beans. Season to taste with salt and pepper.

2. Spread beans in a large deep serving platter. Top with beef.

3. Layer sour cream, olives, chiles, tomatoes, onion, avocado and cheese over beef. Serve with tortilla chips.

Serves 12

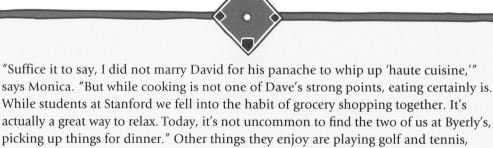

"Suffice it to say, I did not marry David for his panache to whip up 'haute cuisine,'" says Monica. "But while cooking is not one of Dave's strong points, eating certainly is. While students at Stanford we fell into the habit of grocery shopping together. It's actually a great way to relax. Today, it's not uncommon to find the two of us at Byerly's, picking up things for dinner." Other things they enjoy are playing golf and tennis, traveling, and walking their Yorkshire Terrier, Turtle. David says that taking a train trip through Europe to look at castles is his dream vacation. If he weren't playing baseball, he'd like to "play golf all day while my wife works as a lawyer."

8 First Base/ Outfield

Good Catch Vegetable Dip

from Robin and Lenny Webster

This dip tastes better as it ages. Prepare one day before serving.

LINE UP

1 pint mayonnaise
1 pint sour cream
3 tablespoons parsley flakes
1 tablespoon Beau Monde
    seasoning

1 tablespoon dill weed
3 tablespoons minced onion
assorted sliced vegetables such as
    carrots, celery, peppers and
    broccoli

PLAY-BY-PLAY

1. Blend all ingredients except sliced vegetables.

2. Transfer to serving bowl and refrigerate. Serve with sliced vegetables.

Serves 20

Robin says Lenny insists on a side of rice with every meal she cooks. "It doesn't matter if it goes along with the main entrée or not. He has to have it."

23

Gene with Gene Jr., Kelly, and Kathleen

Spinach Squares

from Kathleen and Gene Larkin

LINE UP

1 cup flour
1 teaspoon salt
1 teaspoon baking soda
2 eggs, beaten
1 cup milk

½ cup butter, melted
½ onion, chopped fine
1 pound grated Swiss cheese
10 ounces frozen spinach,
    drained

PLAY-BY-PLAY

1. Preheat oven to 350 degrees. Lightly grease 9-by-13-inch glass baking pan.

2. Combine flour, salt and baking soda. Mix eggs, milk and butter and add to flour mixture.

3. Combine onion, cheese and spinach and add to flour-egg mixture. Spread evenly into baking pan. Bake for 30 minutes, until top is golden.

4. Cool completely and cut into squares.

Serves 12

Bourbon Hot Dogs

from Jana and Jeff Reboulet

> **" A hog dog at the ball park is better than steak at the Ritz. "**
>
> —Humphrey Bogart

LINE UP

1 package hot dogs, cut
  into ½-inch pieces
¾ cup bourbon

1½ cups ketchup
½ cup brown sugar
1 tablespoon grated onion

PLAY-BY-PLAY

1. Place hot dog pieces in 2-quart saucepan. In separate bowl, combine bourbon, ketchup, brown sugar and onion. Mix well.

2. Add bourbon mixture to hot dogs. Bring to a boil, reduce to simmer. Cover and let simmer for 1 hour.

Serves 8

For high school sweethearts Jeff and Jana Reboulet, 1992 was their biggest year— a new home, their first child, Jason, and an adopted Black Lab named Max. To top it all off, Jeff was called up to the majors. They spend the off-seasons in Ohio and enjoy renovating houses. Jeff's secret wish is to be a retired millionaire and "do what I like all day — fish." The Reboulets like watching movies together and taking long walks with Jason and Max. Jana dreams of one day taking Jeff on a luxury tour and Jeff dreams of, well, fishing mostly.

17 **Infielder**

WHO'S WHO

See page 239

Hey
Batter Batter
Breads & Soups

Hey Batter Batter
Breads & Soups

Best Banana Bread

from Eloise and Carl Pohlad

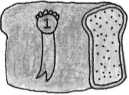

This bread is wonderful! Your guests will not be able to stop eating—the loaf will disappear faster than a home run!

LINE UP

½ cup shortening	1 teaspoon salt
½ cup brown sugar	3 tablespoons buttermilk
½ cup sugar	3 bananas, mashed
2 eggs	¾ cup chopped walnuts,
2 cups sifted flour	if desired
1 teaspoon baking soda	

PLAY-BY-PLAY

1. Preheat oven to 350 degrees. Grease and flour or line 7¼-8¼-by-4-inch loaf pan.

2. Cream shortening and sugars. Add eggs and mix thoroughly.

3. Sift flour with soda and salt. Combine buttermilk and bananas. Fold flour mixture into batter alternately with banana mixture. Do not beat. Stir in walnuts, if desired.

4. Turn batter into loaf pan and bake for 1 hour.

Makes 1 loaf

You can make your own sour milk to substitute for buttermilk. Use the measurement of buttermilk called for in the recipe. Add a few drops of lemon juice to milk and let stand for 5 minutes.

Mather's Muffins

from Shannon and Kevin Mather

Muffin batter will keep in refrigerator for one week.

LINE UP

1 cup honey	2 teaspoons salt
1 cup oil	1½ teaspoons ground ginger
4 eggs	3 tablespoons plus 2 teaspoons
1 quart buttermilk	cinnamon
2½ cups bran flake cereal	1 tablespoon cloves
3 cups flour	3 cups dried fruit, such as
2 cups whole wheat flour	raisins or dates, if desired
1½ cups wheat bran	1 cup chopped walnuts or
1 tablespoon plus 2 teaspoons	pecans, if desired
baking soda	

PLAY-BY-PLAY

1. Preheat oven to 375 degrees. Grease or line muffin tins.

2. Beat together honey, oil, eggs, and buttermilk. Add cereal and let rest 5 minutes.

3. Combine flours, wheat bran, baking soda, salt, ginger, cinnamon and cloves in large mixing bowl. Make a well in the center and pour in cereal mixture. Mix, then add raisins, dates and nuts as desired.

4. Fill muffin tins two-thirds full. Bake for 20 minutes. When done, muffins should spring back when lightly pressed.

Makes 3 dozen large muffins

Kevin and Shannon Mather met when they were both working as CPAs for the same firm. Now they're the proud and busy parents of J.P. (for John Peter) and baby David. The Mathers enjoy spending time together, playing with the children and going to baseball games. Politics and current events are Kevin's favorite interests. He dreams of retiring and running for political office. Kevin's perfect vacation? "Going to the All-Star game with my wife."

VP, Finance

Casian's Cinnamon Rolls

from Michelle and Larry Casian

> **This recipe
> has been a
> Christmas morn-
> ing tradition in
> my family for
> many years.
> Larry and I will
> carry on that
> tradition for
> many more.
> Everyone goes
> for these before
> opening presents.
> There are always
> enough to share
> with friends so
> they can enjoy
> them also. "**
>
> —Michelle Casian

LINE UP

1 package dry yeast
½ cup very warm water
2½ cups sugar
1½ cups warm milk
2 teaspoons salt
2 eggs

½ cup soft shortening
7 cups flour, up to ½ cup more
   as needed
1½ cups butter, melted
¼ cup cinnamon

PLAY-BY-PLAY

1. Proof yeast: Add yeast to water with a pinch of the sugar. Stir gently and set aside for 10 minutes, until foamy. Grease a large bowl.

2. Combine ½ cup of the sugar, milk, salt, eggs, shortening and 3½ cups of the flour with yeast. Mix with spoon until smooth. Mixing with hands, add enough of the remaining flour until dough keeps together and is easy to handle.

3. Turn dough out onto lightly floured board and knead until smooth and elastic, about 5 minutes.

4. Form dough into ball and place in the greased bowl. Turn dough greased side up, cover with a damp cloth. Let rise in a warm, draft-free place for 1½ hours, until dough doubles in bulk.

5. Punch fist into middle of risen dough. Form dough into ball and let rise again until almost double, about 30 minutes.

6. Preheat oven to 350 degrees. Grease four 9-inch baking pans. Combine remaining 2 cups sugar with cinnamon.

7. Separate dough into 1½-inch balls. Roll balls in butter, then in cinnamon sugar. Arrange an inch apart in baking pans. Let rise for 30 minutes.

8. Position pans on top shelf of oven, keeping them away from each other and the sides of the oven. Bake for 20-25 minutes. Invert onto serving platter and enjoy warm from oven.

Makes 4 dozen rolls

Second Base Cinnamon Bread

from Chuck Knoblauch

Chuck, 8 years old

LINE UP

1 cup brown sugar
½ cup sugar
1 tablespoon cinnamon
1 teaspoon allspice
1 cup chopped pecans
½ cup margarine, cut into thin slices
2 12-ounce cans regular-sized refrigerator biscuits

PLAY-BY-PLAY

1. Preheat oven to 350 degrees.

2. Stir together sugars, spices, pecans, and margarine. Chop biscuits into quarters.

3. Combine biscuits and sugar mixture; mix well.

4. Pour into ungreased bundt pan and bake for 30 minutes.

5. Immediately after removing from oven, invert onto serving plate. Pull apart with fingers and enjoy!

Serves 6

One pound (four sticks) of butter or margarine = two cups.
One stick of butter or margarine = ½ cup.

On the Hill Dill Bread

from Sherry and Rick Aguilera

LINE UP

1 package dry yeast
¼ cup warm water
2 tablespoons sugar
1 cup cottage cheese, warmed
1 tablespoon butter
1 teaspoon salt
¼ teaspoon baking soda

1 tablespoon minced onion
2 teaspoons dill seed
1 egg, slightly beaten
2 cups flour, up to ½ cup more
   as needed
2 tablespoons melted butter plus
   a pinch of salt for top

PLAY-BY-PLAY

1. In a small bowl, add yeast to warm water with a pinch of the sugar. Stir to dissolve yeast, then let rest for 10 minutes. Yeast will grow and bubble. Grease 2-quart casserole.

2. In a large bowl, combine the rest of the sugar, cottage cheese, 1 tablespoon butter, salt, and baking soda. Add onion, dill, egg and yeast.

3. Beat well while gradually adding flour. Add more flour if dough seems too sticky. Cover with a damp cloth and let rise in a warm place until doubled, about one hour.

4. Punch down dough and turn into the greased casserole. Let rise again in warm place, 30-40 minutes. Meanwhile, preheat oven to 350 degrees.

5. Bake bread for 35-45 minutes, until crust is golden. Remove from oven. Brush top with melted butter and sprinkle with salt. Cool 5 minutes in casserole, then remove and serve warm.

Makes 1 loaf, serves 6

Gold Glove Garlic Bread

from Mary Ann and Jim Kaat

Bread can be prepared ahead and refrigerated or frozen until use. Bake cold or frozen bread longer, as needed.

❝ Result of Irish mother modifying Italian mother-in-law's recipe. ❞

—Jim Kaat

LINE UP

8 ounces cream cheese, softened
½ cup butter, softened

3 cloves garlic, crushed and minced
1 loaf Italian or French bread

PLAY-BY-PLAY

1. Preheat oven to 350 degrees.

2. Cream together cream cheese and butter. Add garlic.

3. Slice bread diagonally, but not through, so loaf stays intact. Spread both sides of bread slices with mixture, wrap in foil and bake for 25 minutes. Serve hot.

Serves 6

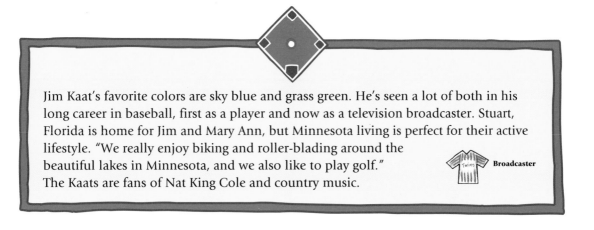

Jim Kaat's favorite colors are sky blue and grass green. He's seen a lot of both in his long career in baseball, first as a player and now as a television broadcaster. Stuart, Florida is home for Jim and Mary Ann, but Minnesota living is perfect for their active lifestyle. "We really enjoy biking and roller-blading around the beautiful lakes in Minnesota, and we also like to play golf." The Kaats are fans of Nat King Cole and country music.

Broadcaster

Grandma Augusta's Gingerbread

from Pat Mahomes

LINE UP

1 cup sugar
1 cup dark molasses
1 cup vegetable oil
2 cups flour
2 eggs
1 cup buttermilk

1 teaspoon nutmeg
1 tablespoon plus 1 teaspoon
   cinnamon
2 teaspoons ground ginger
½ teaspoon baking soda

PLAY-BY-PLAY

1. Preheat oven to 350 degrees. Grease and flour 9-inch square baking pan.

2. Combine all ingredients and mix well. Spread in baking pan and bake for 30 minutes, or until brown and gingerbread pulls away from sides of pan.

Serves 6

In high school, Pat played four sports and was All-State Baseball, All-State Quarterback, Mr. Basketball Texas and ran track. If he weren't playing baseball, he would like to be an NBA basketball player. Lindale, Texas is home to Pat and his family, which includes his brother Eric and sister Tinesha. In his spare time, he likes to golf and play pool. Pat's secret desire is "to play golf in the Bahamas with Michael Jordan and beat him."

20 Pitcher

Mom's Irish Soda Bread

from Kathleen and Gene Larkin

LINE UP

4 cups flour
¼ cup plus 2 tablespoons sugar
1 teaspoon salt
1 teaspoon baking powder
¼ cup margarine

1⅓ cups buttermilk
1 egg
1 teaspoon baking soda
2 tablespoons melted butter

PLAY-BY-PLAY

1. Preheat oven to 375 degrees. Grease a baking sheet.

2. Combine flour, ¼ cup sugar, salt and baking powder. Cut in margarine with a pastry blender or two knives until crumbly.

3. Combine buttermilk, egg and baking soda. Stir into flour mixture until moistened. With hands, knead dough into an 8-inch round and place on baking sheet.

4. Use a sharp knife to cut a deep cross ¼-⅔ of the way through the loaf. Pour melted butter and the remaining 2 tablespoons sugar in the cracks of the cross. Bake for 50-55 minutes.

Serves 8

❝ This favorite recipe is full of tradition. Gene's Mom gave me this recipe— it was passed down to her from her Mom who immigrated to the United States from Ireland. Both sets of Gene's grandparents came here from Ireland. ❞

—Kathleen Larkin

"It's a popover fly-- unbelievable!!"

Herb Carneal's Popovers

from Kathy and Herb Carneal

" If you use Pam cooking spray, these never fail. "

—Kathy Carneal

Even popovers can be made ahead! To reheat, place popovers inside paper bag and fold down to seal. Heat at 350 degrees until hot, about 10 minutes.

LINE UP

1 cup flour
¼ teaspoon salt

2 eggs
1 cup milk

PLAY-BY-PLAY

1. Spray popover tin or muffin tin with non-stick cooking spray. Preheat oven and tin to 400 degrees. Have all ingredients at room temperature.

2. Combine all ingredients, beat for 2 minutes. Fill hot popover cups or muffin cups ⅔ full. Bake for 30 minutes, until crisp. Serve immediately.

Makes 6 popovers, or 12 muffin-sized popovers

World Series Cider Pumpkin Bread

from Nita and Harmon Killebrew

You'll enjoy this bread very much. It seems men like it.

LINE UP

1 cup brown sugar
1 cup canned pumpkin
½ cup oil
½ cup apple cider or apple juice
1 egg
1¾ cups flour
½ cup whole wheat flour

1 tablespoon baking powder
1½ teaspoons cinnamon
½ cup chopped walnuts or pecans
½ cup raisins
8 ounces cream cheese, softened
¼ cup orange marmalade

PLAY-BY-PLAY

1. Preheat oven to 350 degrees. Grease and flour bottom of 9-by-5-inch loaf pan.

2. Combine brown sugar, pumpkin, oil, apple cider and egg in large mixing bowl. Mix well. Add flours, baking powder and cinnamon, stirring just until moistened. Stir in nuts and raisins.

3. Pour batter into loaf pan. Bake for 1 hour, until toothpick inserted in center comes out clean. Cool 10 minutes, then remove bread from pan.

4. Meanwhile, in a small bowl combine cream cheese and orange marmalade. Serve with warm bread. Store bread and spread in refrigerator.

Serves 8

Fast Rising Rolls

from Lori and Jim Deshaies

LINE UP

3 packages dry yeast
¾ cup very warm water
½ cup sugar
½ cup vegetable shortening
2 eggs

¾ cup warm milk
1½ teaspoons salt
2¾ cups whole wheat flour
2¾ cups flour

PLAY-BY-PLAY

1. Combine yeast and water with a pinch of the sugar. Set aside for 10 minutes, until foamy. Grease a large bowl.

2. Cut shortening into remaining sugar. Mix in eggs, milk, salt and yeast. Add flours until dough forms. Turn out onto floured board and knead 5 times.

3. Turn dough into the greased bowl and rotate greased side up. Cover with a damp cloth and let rise in warm draft-free place until doubled in bulk, 1½ hours.

4. Grease 9-by-13-inch baking pan. Punch fist into risen dough then form into 24 balls. Arrange in pan. Cover and let rise 30 minutes. Meanwhile, preheat oven to 400 degrees.

5. Bake rolls for 12-15 minutes, until golden. Turn out onto wire racks. Serve hot.

Makes 24 rolls

Strawberry Bread

from Kathleen and Gene Larkin

LINE UP

3 cups flour
2 cups sugar
1 teaspoon baking soda
1 teaspoon salt
1 teaspoon cinnamon

4 eggs, beaten
¼ cup vegetable oil
20 ounces frozen strawberries,
    drained

PLAY-BY-PLAY

1. Preheat oven to 350 degrees. Grease and flour two 9-by-5-inch loaf pans or five mini-loaf pans.

2. Combine flour, sugar, baking soda, salt and cinnamon. Make a well in the center and stir in eggs, oil and strawberries. Mix well.

3. Pour into prepared loaf pans. Bake 50-60 minutes for large pans, 25 minutes for mini-pans. Cool 10 minutes in pans before removing to wire rack.

Makes two 9-by-5-inch loaves or five mini-loaves

As a newlywed, Gene took two bites of wife Kathleen's first attempt at a gourmet meal and walked out the door. Ten minutes later he returned to his shocked wife with a large cheese pizza in hand. "He said he couldn't find the words to describe how awful the dinner was, so he decided to provide us with something edible," explains Kathleen. Today, the food has improved and life is busy with two children, daughter Kelly and son Gene. Outdoor activities are popular with the Larkins and Gene can't wait until the kids start ice skating. How about Mom? She'll be happy to stand rinkside with a video camera. But no skates.

 Outfield/ First Base

Broadcast Booth Black Bean Soup

from Kathy and Herb Carneal

LINE UP

1 pound black beans
¼ cup olive oil
1 onion, chopped
1 green pepper, chopped
1 bay leaf
1 teaspoon sugar

1 teaspoon oregano
salt and pepper to taste
¼ cup wine
4 cups cooked rice
chopped green onion

PLAY-BY-PLAY

1. Rinse and pick over beans. Place in large stock pot with enough cool water to cover by 3 inches. Simmer until beans are soft, about 2 hours.

2. Meanwhile, heat olive oil in sauté pan and cook onion and green pepper until tender. Add seasonings, sauté 1 minute. Add vegetables and seasonings to simmering beans.

3. Add wine to beans and simmer soup for 20 minutes, until beans are very tender. Serve soup over rice, topped with lots of chopped green onion.

Serves 6-8

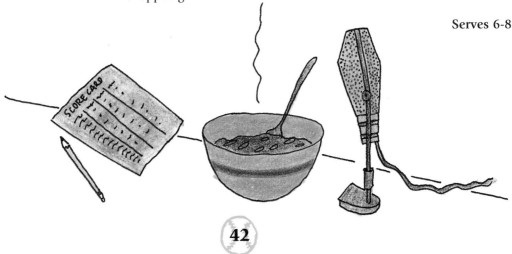

Chicken Chili Blanco

from Sherry and Rick Aguilera

Rick, 10 years old

LINE UP

1 pound dried small
   lima beans, rinsed
6 cups chicken broth
1 teaspoon chicken base,
   or one chicken
   boullion cube
2 onions, chopped
1 tablespoon oil
8 cloves garlic, minced
7 ounces diced green chiles
1 tablespoon ground cumin

2 teaspoons oregano
1 teaspoon cayenne pepper
4 cups diced cooked chicken
1 cup sour cream
3 cups shredded Monterey
   Jack cheese
chopped green onions,
   diced tomatoes,
   chopped cilantro, and
   sour cream

PLAY-BY-PLAY

1. Combine beans, broth and base in large stock pot. Cover and simmer for two hours.

2. Sauté onions in oil until golden.

3. Add onion, garlic, chiles, cumin, oregano, cayenne and chicken to beans. Simmer another 30 minutes. Add sour cream and cheese, heat until cheese melts.

4. Serve with green onions, tomatoes, cilantro, and sour cream as garnishes.

Serves 4-6

*Honeymoon in
Hawaii, 1985*

Chili Herbie-Style

from Jeanie and Kent Hrbek

Jeanie Hrbek serves
this hearty chili with
grated cheese and
sour cream.

LINE UP

2½ pounds ground beef
1 tablespoon oil
2 onions, chopped
1 green pepper, chopped
4 ribs celery, chopped
1 tablespoon garlic powder
1 tablespoon black pepper
2-3 tablespoons chili powder

1 tablespoon plus 1½ teaspoons salt
1 32-ounce can tomatoes, chopped
2 cups tomato juice
1 can tomato soup
1 15.5-ounce can kidney beans
1 tablespoon Worcestershire sauce

PLAY-BY-PLAY

1. In large stock pot, brown beef in oil. Add chopped onions, peppers, and celery; sauté until tender.

2. Add the rest of the ingredients to the pot. Simmer until flavors blend and chili is thick, about 1 hour.

Serves 12-16

Mom's Broccoli Cheese Soup

from Carol and Ron Gardenhire

Cauliflower is a great substitute for broccoli in this quick and flavorful soup.

> **❝ I have my Mom make this for me every time I visit! ❞**
>
> —Carol Gardenhire

LINE UP

¼ cup chopped onion
1 tablespoon margarine
2 cups milk

12 ounces Velveeta cheese, cubed
10 ounces frozen chopped
    broccoli, cooked and drained

PLAY-BY-PLAY

1. In 2-quart saucepan, cook onions in margarine until tender. Add remaining ingredients.

2. Stir over low heat until cheese melts and soup is hot.

Serves 4

Ron and his wife Carol have three children, Toby, Tiffany and Tara. "The kids love being 'baseball kids.' One of their fondest memories is of when Ron was managing in the minor leagues and they would sit with Willie Banks and help him run the radar gun," says Carol. "Toby loves to come to the ballpark with his Dad on Sundays to practice with the team." Ron was hired as the third base coach for the Twins in 1991, after managing in the minor leagues for three years. Carol, a native Minnesotan, was thrilled to be back. Ron's dream vacation is to visit his birthplace in Butzbach, Germany. During the season, the Gardenhires live in Roseville where they have made many good friends.

35 Third Base Coach

Five-Hour-No-Peek Stew

from Eloise and Carl Pohlad

LINE UP

<table>
<tr><td>2 pounds stew meat</td><td>1 28-ounce can tomatoes</td></tr>
<tr><td>8 carrots, diced</td><td>1 cup water</td></tr>
<tr><td>8 ribs celery, diced</td><td>1 teaspoon instant bouillon</td></tr>
<tr><td>4 onions, quartered</td><td>1 tablespoon sugar</td></tr>
<tr><td>6 small potatoes, peeled and cubed</td><td>1 tablespoon salt</td></tr>
<tr><td>1 green pepper, diced</td><td>¼ teaspoon pepper</td></tr>
<tr><td>1 bay leaf, crushed</td><td>1 teaspoon dried basil, crumbled</td></tr>
<tr><td>⅓ cup instant tapioca</td><td>1 teaspoon minced garlic</td></tr>
</table>

PLAY-BY-PLAY

1. Preheat oven to 250 degrees.

2. Combine all ingredients in 3-quart casserole. Cover and bake for 5 hours.

Serves 8

❝ Don't peek while cooking; it will be brown, juicy, done and delicious! ❞

—Carl Pohlad

Old-Fashioned Potato Soup

from Cori and Pat Meares

LINE UP

5 potatoes, peeled and diced
2 ribs celery, diced
2 tablespoons margarine
2 tablespoons flour

1 cup milk
½ teaspoon salt
1 small onion, minced

PLAY-BY-PLAY

1. Cook potatoes and celery in small amount of water over low heat until tender. Drain.

2. Melt margarine over low heat. Add flour, stirring until smooth. Slowly add milk, stirring constantly to keep mixture smooth. Keep stirring until sauce thickens. Add salt and onion. Keep on low heat.

3. Add vegetables to white sauce. Continue to cook over low until heated thoroughly.

Serves 4

❝ Serve during the cold winter months to warm yourself. Great with crackers and sandwiches. ❞

—Cori Meares

Strike Out Salmon Soup

from Sharon and Kevin Tapani

❝ One of the few things besides burgers and brats that Kevin asked me to make. ❞

—Kevin's Mom, Sandy

LINE UP

6 potatoes, cubed
1 cup sliced carrots
½ cup thinly sliced celery
1 tablespoon salt
3 cups water
10 ounces frozen peas

1 1-pound can pink or red salmon
⅓ cup margarine
⅓ cup chopped onion
¼ cup flour
5 cups milk
½ teaspoon Worcestershire sauce

PLAY-BY-PLAY

1. In large saucepan, combine potatoes, carrots, celery, 1 teaspoon of the salt and water. Cover and cook over medium heat until tender. Add peas and bring to boil. Remove from heat; do not drain. Cool one minute.

2. Skin and bone salmon, reserving liquid. Add fish and liquid to vegetables.

3. Melt margarine in sauté pan, add onions and sauté over medium heat until golden. Reduce heat and add flour, stir until smooth. Cook one minute and add 2½ cups milk, stirring constantly. Cook over low heat until mixture bubbles and thickens.

4. Add hot white sauce, Worcestershire sauce and remaining 2½ cups milk to vegetable-salmon mixture. Season with remaining salt. Heat thoroughly and serve at once.

Serves 12 (3 quarts)

Venison Stew

from Sue and Terry Jorgensen

This is my sister-in-law Sherry's recipe.

LINE UP

1½ pounds venison stew meat
salt and pepper to taste
1 1-ounce package dry onion
*   soup mix*
1 can cream of mushroom soup
1 soup can water

2 tablespoons ketchup or
*   tomato paste*
¼ cup wine
3 potatoes, peeled
2 ribs celery
3 carrots, peeled

PLAY-BY-PLAY

1. Preheat oven to 300 degrees. Brown venison. Season to taste with salt and pepper. Place in large roasting pan.

2. Add soup mix, soup, water, ketchup and wine to roasting pan. Bake for 2½ hours.

3. Cut potatoes, celery, and carrots into 1-inch pieces and add to stew. Bake for 1 hour.

Serves 6

Terry, Brent, and Sue

Red River Chili

from Bob Dorey

LINE UP

3 pounds beef round or chuck, cut into ½-inch cubes
¼ cup vegetable oil
1 onion, chopped fine
1 clove garlic, minced
1 28-ounce can plum tomatoes, chopped
1 13¾-ounce can beef broth

1 4½-ounce can diced green chiles
1 teaspoon celery seed, crushed
1 teaspoon cumin seed, crushed
1 tablespoon chili powder, or to taste
1 teaspoon salt
2 15.5-ounce cans red kidney beans, drained

PLAY-BY-PLAY

1. In a large kettle or dutch oven, brown beef, part at a time, in 2 tablespoons of the vegetable oil. As it browns, remove beef from kettle.

2. In the same kettle, sauté onion and garlic in remaining 2 tablespoons oil until tender, about 3 minutes.

3. Return browned beef to kettle with tomatoes, broth, chiles and spices. Bring to a boil. Lower heat and simmer, stirring occasionally, for 3 hours, until meat is tender. Taste for seasoning.

4. Add kidney beans to chili and cook for 15 more minutes.

Serves 10

 If the chili seems dry as it simmers, add tomato juice.

Wild Rice Soup

from Marge and Jim Wiesner

Not for those with high cholesterol! You can substitute lowfat ingredients, but it's not as good. Great for after-sports activities in the winter.

LINE UP

4 cups water
½ cup wild rice, rinsed very well and drained
1 onion, minced
2 tablespoons butter or margarine

1 quart milk
2 cans cream of potato soup
1 pound Velveeta cheese, cubed
10 strips cooked bacon, crumbled

PLAY-BY-PLAY

1. Bring 2 cups of the water to a boil in a covered saucepan. Slowly stir in wild rice and return to a boil. Reduce heat and cover. Simmer for 40 minutes. Fluff with a fork. If any water remains, simmer uncovered for 5 minutes and fluff again. Set cooked rice aside.

2. In a large saucepan, sauté onion in butter over low heat until tender, about 10 minutes. Add remaining 2 cups water, milk and soup. Increase heat to medium, stirring occasionally.

3. When soup is hot, stir in cheese. Cook and stir until melted and creamy. Add wild rice and bacon. Heat thoroughly and serve.

Serves 6-8

❝ How we met? I was a secretary for the Minnesota Twins and Jim was manager of the visiting clubhouse. ❞

—Marge Wiesner

 You can substitute chopped ham for the crumbled bacon.

WHO'S WHO

10

11

12

13

See page 239

Play Ball!
Main Courses

Play Ball! Main Courses

Seaside Beef and Broccoli
Chow Mein
56

Larry's Favorite
Beef Enchiladas
57

Championship Chili Pie
58

Cheeseburger Pie
59

Power Alley Pot Roast
60

One-Two-Three Kabobs
61

Metrodome Meatloaf
62

Bob's Secret Chili Sauce
63

Italian Meatloaf
64

Mini-Meatloaves
65

Holy Cow!
Oven Steak and Veggies
66

Spanish Rice
67

Killebrew Strobalaugh
68

Pittsburgh Stroganoff
69

Shortstop Beef Casserole
70

Chuck Knob-Broccoli
Casserole
71

Chicken and Broccoli
Casserole
72

"Can o' Corn" Casserole
73

Big Hit Carrot Casserole
74

Hip Hooray Huntington
Chicken Casserole
75

Hit and Run
Ham and Noodle Casserole
76

Hot Hash Brown
Potato Casserole
77

Play at the Plate
Spinach Casserole
78

Winner's Wild Rice
Casserole
79

First Round Pick
Steak Casserole
80

Puck's BBQ Chicken
81

Fowl Ball Fettucine Alfredo
82

Chicken Intrigue
83

Tapani's Tasty Chicken
and Biscuits
84

Chicken Fricassé à la Petey
85

It's Outta Here!
Chicken Chili
86

Chicken That Makes
Its Own Gravy
87

Pay-Off Pitch
Parmesan Chicken
88

Pennant Chase
Paprika Chicken
89

Cheddar Chicken Risotto
90

Slugger's Sautéed Chicken
91

Twig's Spiced Chicken
92

Play Ball! Main Courses

Seaside Beef and Broccoli Chow Mein

from Lori and Jim Deshaies

LINE UP

1¾ pound very lean beef,
    cut diagonally into
    1½-by-¼-inch strips
2 tablespoons soy sauce
1 clove garlic, minced
2 tablespoons plus 1½ teaspoons
    cornstarch
1 teaspoon grated fresh ginger
dash cayenne pepper
½ cup dry sherry, if desired

1½ cups beef broth
¼ cup plus 1 tablespoon
    peanut oil
¼ cup chopped green onions
8 ounces fresh bay scallops
8 ounces fresh broccoli florets
2 tablespoons water
1 8½-ounce can sliced
    water chestnuts, drained
13 ounces chow mein noodles

Be careful not to use ground ginger in place of fresh ginger. Used for baking, ground ginger does not have the same spicy-sweet flavors as fresh. You'll find fresh ginger in the produce department. Just break off a small knob and peel before using as directed in your recipe.

PLAY-BY-PLAY

1. In medium bowl, combine beef, soy sauce and garlic. Marinate for at least 15 minutes. Should be at room temperature before cooking.

2. In another bowl, combine cornstarch, ginger, cayenne, sherry and broth. Set aside.

3. Heat 2 tablespoons of the peanut oil in wok over high heat. Add beef and green onion. Stir-fry until brown. Remove meat.

4. Add 1 more tablespoon peanut oil to wok, heat and add scallops. Stir-fry 1-2 minutes, until scallops are opaque. Remove scallops.

5. Add remaining 2 tablespoons peanut oil to wok, heat and add broccoli. Stir-fry 1 minute. Add water and water chestnuts. Cover and cook 3 minutes. Add cornstarch mixture, beef, and scallops. Stir-fry until sauce thickens and beef and scallops are well-heated. Serve over chow mein noodles.

Serves 6-8

Larry's Favorite Beef Enchiladas

from Michelle and Larry Casian

Dating, 1987

LINE UP

1 pound ground beef
1 4¼-ounce can chopped
    black olives
2 10-ounce cans enchilada sauce

8 ounces American cheese, grated
8 ounces cheddar cheese, grated
12 corn tortillas
½ cup corn oil

PLAY-BY-PLAY

1. Preheat oven to 350 degrees.

2. Brown beef, add chopped olives. Heat corn oil in sauté pan. Turn heat to low and heat each tortilla in oil until soft.

3. Mix half of each cheese with beef and olive mixture and half the enchilada sauce.

4. Roll cheese, beef and enchilada sauce mixture into each tortilla and secure with toothpick. Arrange in baking dish.

5. Spread remaining enchilada sauce over all. Cover with remaining cheese and bake for 30 minutes.

Serves 4-6

❝ This is Larry's favorite recipe. He likes it best the next day. ❞

—Michelle Casian

Championship Chili Pie

from Eloise and Carl Pohlad

LINE UP

2 pounds lean ground beef
1 large onion, chopped
salt and pepper to taste
12 flour tortillas, torn in fourths
1 can cream of mushroom soup
1 can cream of chicken soup

1 10-ounce can hot enchilada
   sauce
1 cup milk
1 4½-ounce can chopped green
   chiles
12 ounces shredded cheddar
   cheese

PLAY-BY-PLAY

1. Preheat oven to 350 degrees.

2. Brown beef with onion, pour off fat. Season with salt and pepper. Combine soups, enchilada sauce and milk.

3. Line lasagna pan or large rectangular baking pan with half of the tortilla fourths. Layer with half of the beef, then pour half of the soup mixture over all. Repeat layers.

4. Top casserole with cheese and bake for 30 minutes.

Serves 4-6

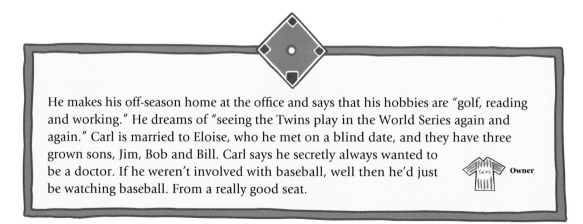

He makes his off-season home at the office and says that his hobbies are "golf, reading and working." He dreams of "seeing the Twins play in the World Series again and again." Carl is married to Eloise, who he met on a blind date, and they have three grown sons, Jim, Bob and Bill. Carl says he secretly always wanted to be a doctor. If he weren't involved with baseball, well then he'd just be watching baseball. From a really good seat.

Owner

Cheeseburger Pie

from Marge and Jim Wiesner

LINE UP

2 pounds ground beef, browned
½ teaspoon oregano
scant teaspoon salt
pepper to taste
1 onion, chopped
1 green pepper, chopped

1 cup bread crumbs
2 15-ounce cans tomato sauce
2 9-inch pie crusts
1 pound grated cheddar cheese
2 eggs
⅓ cup milk

❝ Men love this, kids too! ❞

—Marge Wiesner

PLAY-BY-PLAY

1. Preheat oven to 425 degrees.

2. Combine beef, oregano, salt, pepper, onion, green pepper, bread crumbs and tomato sauce. Mix well and divide between pie crusts, using about 3 cups for each.

3. Combine cheddar, eggs and milk. Mix well and spread over top of pies.

4. Bake pies for 15 minutes. Reduce oven temperature to 350 and bake for 30 minutes longer.

Serves 12, each pie serves 6

Marge Wiesner can't imagine not being involved with baseball — "There is no other life!" She and Jim met when she was a secretary for the Twins and Jim was the manager of the visiting clubhouse. They got married and life has been a baseball affair ever since. During their career with the Twins, Marge and Jim have raised two children, Barb and T.J. Marge enjoys traveling, playing golf, shopping (especially at the Mall of America) and gardening. Her secret wish? "To be a backup singer (but I can't really sing) for a very famous group or solo singer. Michael Bolton or Jon Secada would be fine."

Equipment Manager

Power Alley Pot Roast

from Kathleen and Gene Larkin

Every week during spring training in Fort Myers, Aunt Kathy and Uncle Harry invite us over for some good home cooking. Uncle Harry is a great Italian cook, but Aunt Kathy's pot roast won Gene's vote. I make this all the time for those cold Minnesota evenings. The aroma fills the house with that homey feeling.

LINE UP

1 1½-ounce package dry onion soup mix

1 can cream of mushroom soup

1 can cream of asparagus soup

1 top or bottom beef round roast

PLAY-BY-PLAY

1. Combine soup mix with soups in 5½-quart crock pot. Add roast and let cook all day, 6-8 hours. Remove roast to serving platter.

2. Strain cooking juices, skim off fat. Simmer cooking juices in saucepan until juices thicken to gravy. Slice roast and serve with gravy.

Serves 4

One-Two-Three Kabobs

from Danielle and Derek Parks

These hot-off-the-grill kabobs go great with grilled corn on the cob and baked or grilled potatoes.

LINE UP

*1 pound top sirloin steak,
    cubed large*
*1 pound boneless chicken breast,
    cubed large*
1 onion, cut into large pieces

*1 green pepper, cut into
    large pieces*
8 mushrooms
garlic salt

PLAY-BY-PLAY

1. Preheat grill or broiler.

2. Alternate all ingredients on skewers. Sprinkle with garlic salt. Grill or broil until done to taste.

Serves 4-6

*Derek, Danielle,
Ashley, and Chelsea*

Metrodome Meatloaf

from Bob Dorey

LINE UP

2 pounds lean ground beef
1 egg
25 saltine crackers, crushed

1 cup Bob's Secret Chili Sauce
(see page 63)
salt and pepper to taste

PLAY-BY-PLAY

1. Preheat oven to 375 degrees.

2. Combine all ingredients and mix well. Form into loaf shape and place in meatloaf pan or 9-by-5-inch loaf pan.

3. Bake meatloaf for 30-40 minutes. If you used a regular loaf pan, drain off fat before serving.

Serves 4-6

Bob's Secret Chili Sauce

from Bob Dorey

LINE UP

4 dry quarts ripe tomatoes
1 small onion, chopped
¾ cup chopped red and
    green pepper
1 rib celery, chopped
½ cup plus 2 tablespoons sugar

½ cup plus 2 tablespoons
    brown sugar
½ cup vinegar
2 tablespoons salt
½ teaspoon cinnamon
½ teaspoon cloves
½ teaspoon nutmeg

You can use 4
28-ounce cans of
whole tomatoes in
place of fresh ripe
tomatoes. Just drain,
dice and cook as
directed in the recipe.

PLAY-BY-PLAY

1. Peel tomatoes by dropping them into boiling water, letting stand for a minute, draining, and slipping off the skins. Dice tomatoes and drain again.

2. Bring tomatoes to a boil in a large saucepan and simmer until thick. Add onion, peppers and celery. Simmer until fairly tender but not mushy, about 25 minutes.

3. Add sugars, vinegar, salt and spices. Heat to boiling. Simmer for 10 more minutes. Use immediately or freeze in 1-pint containers.

Makes 4 pints chili sauce

Italian Meatloaf

from Shannon and Kevin Mather

Meatloaf pans have holes in the bottom and an extra sleeve for drainage. If you don't have one, use a regular loaf pan and pour off any fat before serving.

" A family favorite. "

—Shannon Mather

LINE UP

1½ pounds ground beef
¾ cup seasoned bread crumbs
¾ cup plus ⅓ cup spaghetti sauce
1 small onion, chopped

1 egg
½ teaspoon garlic powder
¼ teaspoon salt
¼ teaspoon pepper

PLAY-BY-PLAY

1. Preheat oven to 350 degrees.

2. Combine beef, bread crumbs, ¾ cup spaghetti sauce, onion, egg and seasonings. Spread into meatloaf pan or 9-by-5-inch loaf pan. Top with remaining ⅓ cup spaghetti sauce.

3. Cover with foil and bake for 45 minutes. Uncover and bake for another 45 minutes.

Serves 6

Mini-Meatloaves

from Barbara and Mike Trombley

> " Mike and I met when I was a sophomore and he was a freshman at Duke University. I was tentative about dating a freshman until I found out that Mike was two days older than me. "
>
> —Barbara Trombley

LINE UP

1½ pounds lean ground beef
1 small onion, chopped
1 egg
¼ cup bread crumbs
salt and pepper to taste

1 tablespoon olive oil
2 8-ounce cans tomato sauce
¼ cup ketchup
dash Worcestershire sauce
¼ cup warm water

PLAY-BY-PLAY

1. Combine beef, onion, egg, bread crumbs, and salt and pepper. Mix well and form into six miniature loaves like oval meatballs.

2. Heat olive oil in large sauté pan and brown mini-loaves.

3. Add tomato sauce, ketchup, Worcestershire and water. Cover and simmer for 20 minutes.

Serves 6

Holy Cow!
Oven Steak and Veggies

from Danielle and Derek Parks

LINE UP

¼ cup flour
salt and pepper to taste
self-sealing plastic bag
1½ pounds beef round steak,
   cubed large

2 tablespoons oil
1 16-ounce can tomatoes
1 small onion, chopped
4 carrots, sliced into strips
4 cups cooked rice

PLAY-BY-PLAY

1. Preheat oven to 350 degrees. Combine flour and salt and pepper in self-sealing plastic bag. Add beef and shake well to coat.

2. Brown beef in hot oil. Remove to 2-quart casserole. Stir remaining seasoned flour into pan drippings along with tomatoes and their juice, and onion. Cook, stirring, until sauce bubbles and thickens.

3. Pour sauce over meat. Add carrots, cover and bake for 1 hour. Check for seasoning and serve over rice.

Serves 6

Spanish Rice

from Judi and Chip Hale

LINE UP

1 tablespoon olive oil	1 teaspoon garlic powder
1 onion, diced	1 tablespoon parsley flakes
1 green pepper, diced	salt and pepper to taste
1 red pepper, diced	1 teaspoon cumin
2 pounds ground beef	dash cayenne pepper
1 8-ounce can tomato sauce	1 cup mild salsa
⅔ cup water	2 cups Minute rice

PLAY-BY-PLAY

1. Heat olive oil in large saucepan. Sauté onion and peppers until tender. Add beef and cook until done.

2. Add tomato sauce, water, spices and salsa to pan. Simmer 10 minutes.

3. Add rice to saucepan. If mixture looks dry, add a little more water. Cover and cook on low for 10 more minutes.

Serves 6-8

Killebrew Strobalaugh

from Nita and Harmon Killebrew

LINE UP

❝ Feeds an army! ❞

—Harmon Killebrew

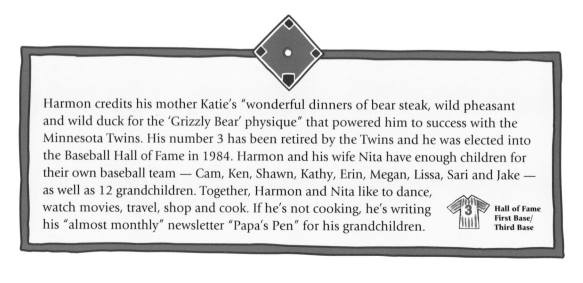

You can also add pre-cooked miniature shrimp to the sauté with the vegetables.

2 large onions, chopped
2 large green peppers, chopped
2 tablespoons butter
4 pounds lean ground sirloin
2 28-ounce cans stewed tomatoes
2 teaspoons salt
2 teaspoons pepper
2 tablespoons Worchestershire sauce
4 cups cooked rice

PLAY-BY-PLAY

1. Sauté onions and peppers in butter. Drain and set aside.

2. In large sauté pan, brown beef over high heat. Drain off excess fat. Add sautéed vegetables and stewed tomatoes. Heat thoroughly.

3. Season to taste with salt, pepper and Worchestershire sauce. Add rice, cover and cook over low heat until hot. Transfer to a large casserole and serve.

Serves 10-12

Harmon credits his mother Katie's "wonderful dinners of bear steak, wild pheasant and wild duck for the 'Grizzly Bear' physique" that powered him to success with the Minnesota Twins. His number 3 has been retired by the Twins and he was elected into the Baseball Hall of Fame in 1984. Harmon and his wife Nita have enough children for their own baseball team — Cam, Ken, Shawn, Kathy, Erin, Megan, Lissa, Sari and Jake — as well as 12 grandchildren. Together, Harmon and Nita like to dance, watch movies, travel, shop and cook. If he's not cooking, he's writing his "almost monthly" newsletter "Papa's Pen" for his grandchildren.

3 **Hall of Fame**
First Base/
Third Base

Pittsburgh Stroganoff

from Lark and Andy MacPhail

Whether you're making dinner for the family or feeding the whole team, this recipe works beautifully. Double it or triple it as you need to, then sit back and watch the crowd go wild.

LINE UP

3 pounds boneless beef, cubed
3 cans cream of mushroom soup
1½ cups dry sherry

1 1½-ounce package dry onion soup mix
4 cups cooked rice or 1 pound cooked noodles

PLAY-BY-PLAY

1. Preheat oven to 350 degrees.

2. Combine all ingredients except rice or noodles in 2½-quart casserole.

3. Cover and bake for 3 hours. Serve over rice or noodles.

Serves 6-8

Lark, Andy, William, and Andrew

Shortstop Beef Casserole

from Cori and Pat Meares

❝ This Mexican dish was brought to my mother's bridal shower as a gift when she married my father. Mom fixed it all these years for her husband, and now I am cooking it for *mine*. ❞

—Cori Meares

LINE UP

1 pound ground beef
1 small onion, chopped
1 clove garlic, minced
1 8-ounce can tomato sauce
¼ teaspoon oregano
1 tablespoon chili powder

1 15.5-ounce can kidney beans
   and juice
8 ounces corn chips, crushed
8 ounces grated cheddar cheese
3 tomatoes, chopped
½ head lettuce, chopped
hot sauce

PLAY-BY-PLAY

1. Brown beef, onion and garlic. Stir in tomato sauce and seasonings.

2. Layer meat, beans and chips twice into 2-quart casserole. Microwave on medium heat for 6 minutes.

3. Top with cheese, tomatoes and lettuce. Serve with hot sauce.

Serves 6

Chuck Knob-Broccoli Casserole

from Chuck Knoblauch

LINE UP

1 pound boneless, skinless
   chicken
salt and pepper to taste
1 can cream of mushroom soup
8 ounces Cheese Whiz

10 ounces frozen broccoli,
   slightly steamed
2 cups cooked rice
6 ounces sliced cheddar cheese

PLAY-BY-PLAY

1. Preheat oven to 350 degrees. Cut chicken into 1½-inch pieces. Sauté and season with salt and pepper.

2. Combine soup and Cheese Whiz, mix well. Add chicken, broccoli and rice and place into 1½-quart casserole. Arrange sliced cheese over top.

3. Cover and bake for 30 minutes.

Serves 4-6

❝ This is Chuck's favorite recipe. I always make it when he comes home or when we are together. During the 1991 World Series, I made this for him—the cameras recorded it. ❞

—Chuck's mom
Linda

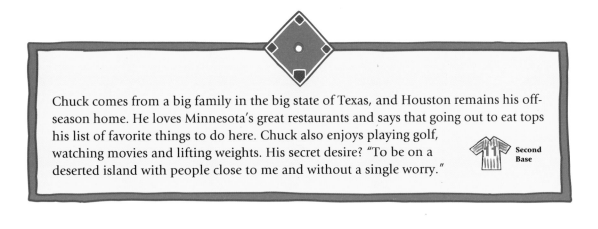

Chuck comes from a big family in the big state of Texas, and Houston remains his off-season home. He loves Minnesota's great restaurants and says that going out to eat tops his list of favorite things to do here. Chuck also enjoys playing golf, watching movies and lifting weights. His secret desire? "To be on a deserted island with people close to me and without a single worry."

11 Second Base

Chicken and Broccoli Casserole

from Rachel and Carl Willis

LINE UP

½ cup butter
2 cups diced celery
1 green pepper, diced
8 ounces fresh mushrooms, sliced
1 pound fresh broccoli, chopped
1 onion, diced
1¼ pounds diced cooked chicken

1 tablespoon salt
1 teaspoon pepper
¼ teaspoon garlic salt
1 pound cream cheese, softened
8 ounces shredded cheddar or
    Monterey Jack cheese

❝ This is one of Carl's favorite dishes. ❞

—Rachel Willis

PLAY-BY-PLAY

1. Preheat oven to 350 degrees. Grease 9-by-13-inch glass baking dish.

2. Melt butter in large sauté pan and cook vegetables until tender. Add chicken and seasonings.

3. Add cream cheese to sauté and blend over low heat until cheese melts. Pour into baking dish and bake for 30 minutes, until top is golden brown.

4. Top casserole with shredded cheese and return to oven to brown again, about 10 minutes.

Serves 6-8

"Can o' Corn" Casserole

from Michelle and Larry Casian

LINE UP

1 pound ground beef
12 ounces elbow macaroni,
*   cooked*

1 14½-ounce can corn
1 16-ounce can tomato sauce
1 pound Velveeta, sliced thin

PLAY-BY-PLAY

1. Preheat oven to 350 degrees.

2. Brown ground beef in sauté pan. Drain off fat. Combine with macaroni, corn and tomato sauce.

3. In 2-quart casserole, layer beef mixture with cheese slices. Repeat, topping with cheese.

4. Bake for 30 minutes, until bubbling.

Serves 6

Big Hit Carrot Casserole

from Sharon and Kevin Tapani

LINE UP

2 pounds sliced carrots
1 can cream of celery soup
1 cup grated cheddar cheese

⅓ cup wheat germ
¼ cup dry bread crumbs
3 tablespoons melted butter

PLAY-BY-PLAY

1. Preheat oven to 350 degrees. Spray 1-quart casserole with non-stick cooking spray.

2. Place carrots in casserole. Top with soup, cheese, wheat germ and bread crumbs. Drizzle with melted butter. Bake for 1 hour.

Serves 6-8

❦ Great way to get kids to eat carrots. ❞

—Sharon Tapani

Hip Hooray Huntington Chicken Casserole

from Carol and Ron Gardenhire

LINE UP

1 tablespoon butter
1 tablespoon flour
1 cup milk
1 can cream of mushroom soup
8 ounces Velveeta cheese, cubed
7 ounces macaroni, cooked and
    drained
1½ cups chopped cooked chicken
salt and pepper to taste
⅓ cup bread crumbs

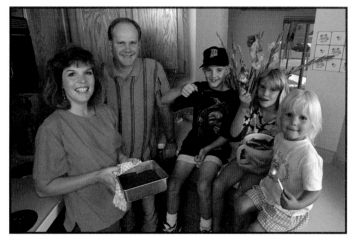

Carol, Ron, Toby,
Tiffany and Tara

PLAY-BY-PLAY

1. Preheat oven to 350 degrees.

2. Melt butter over low heat. Add flour, whisking constantly. Cook gently until golden. Gradually add milk and soup, whisking until sauce is thick.

3. Add cheese to sauce, cook until melted, stirring constantly. Remove from heat. Stir in macaroni, chicken and salt and pepper. Turn mixture into 1½-quart casserole.

4. Top casserole with bread crumbs and bake for 1 hour.

Serves 4 hungry men

This is a recipe that even the kids will love. You will too because it's so easy to put together.

Wedding, 1990

Hit and Run Ham and Noodle Casserole

from Donna and Greg Brummett

LINE UP

24 ounces egg noodles, cooked and drained
2 pounds chopped ham
2 cans cream of mushroom soup
2 cans cheddar cheese soup
1 small onion, chopped
salt and pepper to taste
¾ cup crumbled potato chips

PLAY-BY-PLAY

1. Preheat oven to 350 degrees. Grease 2½-quart casserole.

2. Combine noodles with ham, soups, onion and salt and pepper. Mix well and pour into casserole.

3. Sprinkle casserole with potato chips and bake for 1 hour.

Serves 6-8

Hot Hash Brown Potato Casserole

from Diane and Dick Martin

LINE UP

2 pounds frozen hash browns
10 ounces finely grated cheddar
    cheese
1 teaspoon salt
½ teaspoon pepper

1 small onion, chopped
1 can cream of chicken soup
1 cup sour cream
½ cup melted butter
¾ cup bread crumbs

PLAY-BY-PLAY

1. Preheat oven to 350 degrees. Grease 9-by-13-inch glass baking dish.

2. Combine frozen hash browns, cheese, salt, pepper, onion, soup, sour cream and ¼ cup of the melted butter. Pour into baking dish.

3. Combine remaining ¼ cup melted butter with bread crumbs and sprinkle over top of casserole. Bake for 1 hour and 10 minutes.

Serves 12

You may find Dick and Diane Martin on the road to discover the American West or on an island in the South Pacific. But chances are, wherever you find Dick, he'll be fishing. His hobbies include fly-tying, hunting, running and tennis. The Martins make their off-season home in West Melbourne, Florida with their teenagers Laura and Ty.

Head Athletic Trainer

Brian, with Lance, Chris, Brett, and Derek

Play at the Plate Spinach Casserole

from Chris and Brian Harper

❝ This side dish never lacks for compliments. Brian's sister Sharon gave it to us in 1980. I have passed it on many times. You can substitute broccoli for spinach, but we like spinach best. You'll love it! ❞

—Chris Harper

LINE UP

20 ounces frozen spinach, thawed and drained
2 cups cottage cheese
2 cups cubed cheddar cheese

1 teaspoon salt
¼ cup flour
4 eggs
½ cup butter, cubed

PLAY-BY-PLAY

1. Preheat oven to 300 degrees.
2. Combine all ingredients in 2-quart casserole.
3. Bake uncovered for 1 hour.

Serves 6-8

Winner's Wild Rice Casserole

from Kathy and Herb Carneal

This casserole can be prepared ahead, frozen, and reheated. Serve with a jello salad and a good dessert.

LINE UP

2½ pounds veal and pork for
    chow mein
1 large onion, chopped
4 ribs celery, chopped
1 cup wild rice
1 can cream of mushroom soup
1 can cream of chicken soup
½ cup chopped green pepper

1 4-ounce can mushrooms,
    drained
¼ cup water
½ cup milk
1 2-ounce jar pimentos
tabasco sauce to taste
½ cup cashews

❝ Great for a shower or church supper. ❞

—Kathy Carneal

PLAY-BY-PLAY

1. Preheat oven to 350 degrees. Brown meat with onion and celery.

2. Combine meat and vegetables with rice, soups, green pepper, mushrooms, water, milk, pimentos and tabasco sauce. Pour into 2½-quart casserole.

3. Bake casserole for 2 hours, stirring 3-4 times during second hour. Add more milk and water if the casserole seems too thick. Top with cashews for the last 20 minutes of cooking time.

Serves 10-12

First Round Pick Steak Casserole

from Karilyn and Terry Ryan

Terry Ryan, Vice President of Player Personnel, is a former pitcher who was drafted by the Twins.

LINE UP

2 pounds ground beef
1 large onion, chopped
1 large green pepper, chopped
1 6-ounce can tomato paste
1 can tomato soup
1 4-ounce can mushrooms, drained

1 4-ounce jar pimento-stuffed olives, drained and cut in thirds
2 cups cooked small shell pasta
12 ounces Velveeta cheese, cubed

PLAY-BY-PLAY

1. Preheat oven to 350 degrees.

2. Sauté beef, onion and pepper until beef is brown and onions are golden.

3. Add tomato paste and soup, mushrooms, olives and pasta. Place in 2-quart casserole. Top with Velveeta and bake for 45 minutes.

Serves 4-6

Puck's BBQ Chicken

from Tonya and Kirby Puckett

LINE UP

4 pieces boneless, skinless
   chicken breast
salt and pepper to taste
3 large carrots, sliced
1 red pepper, sliced

1 green pepper, sliced
1 zucchini, sliced
3 ribs celery, sliced
1½ cups hickory-smoked
   barbecue sauce

PLAY-BY-PLAY

1. Preheat oven to 375 degrees. Rinse and pat dry chicken, arrange in baking pan. Sprinkle with salt and pepper.

2. Lay vegetables over chicken. Cover and bake for 40 minutes. Spread barbecue sauce over all and bake uncovered for 15 more minutes.

Serves 4

Goes great with corn on the cob and tossed salad.

Tonya, Kirby, Kirby Jr., and Catherine

81

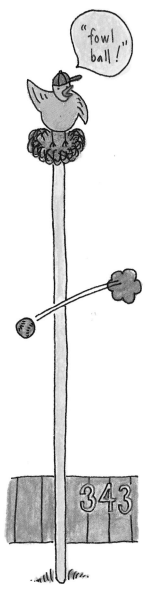

Fowl Ball Fettucine Alfredo

from Sharon and Kevin Tapani

Tap is a big pasta eater on game day. This fettucine is good for a few strikes. The recipe is easy and tastes great—try Pasta Prima or Knorr's Alfredo sauce.

LINE UP

¼ cup butter
¼ cup virgin olive oil
1 pound boneless, skinless
    chicken, cubed
4 green onions, chopped
2 cloves garlic, minced
1 cup half and half
1 package alfredo sauce mix

1 15-ounce can tomatoes
salt and pepper to taste
¼ cup chopped fresh parsley
2 tablespoons chopped fresh basil
8 ounces fettucine, cooked and
    drained
½ cup freshly grated parmesan
    cheese

PLAY-BY-PLAY

1. Combine butter and olive oil in heavy sauté pan over medium heat. When hot, add chicken, onion and garlic and sauté until chicken is golden.

2. Stir in half and half, sauce mix, tomatoes and salt and pepper to taste. Turn heat up to high and bring mixture to a boil. Reduce heat to medium and simmer until sauce is thick, 3-5 minutes.

3. Stir parsley and basil into sauce. Remove from heat. Toss sauce with pasta and serve, sprinkled with parmesan.

Serves 4-6

Chicken Intrigue

from Lark and Andy MacPhail

LINE UP

6 skinless chicken breasts
1 1½-ounce package dry onion
   soup mix

8 ounces Russian salad dressing
8 ounces apricot preserves

PLAY-BY-PLAY

1. Preheat oven to 350 degrees.

2. Arrange chicken in a single layer in shallow casserole.
Combine remaining ingredients and spoon over the chicken.

3. Bake chicken for 1 hour.

Serves 6

Tapani's Tasty Chicken and Biscuits

from Sharon and Kevin Tapani

High School Prom, 1982

LINE UP

10 ounces frozen peas, rinsed and drained
2 cups cooked chicken, cubed
1 can cream of chicken soup
½ cup sour cream
½ cup milk
½ teaspoon salt
dash pepper
1¼ cups shredded cheddar cheese
1 can refrigerator buttermilk biscuits

PLAY-BY-PLAY

1. Preheat oven to 425 degrees.

2. Heat peas, chicken, soup, sour cream, milk, salt and pepper to just boiling, stirring frequently. Reduce heat and keep warm.

3. Pour chicken mixture into 2-quart casserole. Sprinkle with cheese.

4. Place biscuits over cheese. Bake until biscuits are golden, 20 minutes.

Serves 4

Chicken Fricassé à la Petey

from Pedro Muñoz

LINE UP

1 3-pound chicken
1 tablespoon salt
½ teaspoon pepper
2 cloves garlic, minced
½ teaspoon oregano
1 tablespoon vinegar
½ cup vegetable oil
½ cup tomato sauce
1 tablespoon capers

1 bay leaf
2 red peppers, sliced
1 small onion, sliced
½ cup pimento-stuffed
　green olives
4 ounces chopped cooked ham
1 pound potatoes, peeled
　and cubed

PLAY-BY-PLAY

1. Rinse chicken and pat dry. Cut into serving pieces. Sprinkle with salt, pepper, garlic and oregano. Refrigerate for 2-3 hours.

2. Combine vinegar, oil, tomato sauce, capers and bay leaf in large sauté pan. Add chicken, peppers, onion, olives and ham. Cover and cook over low heat until heated through, stirring occasionally.

3. Add potatoes to pan and cook until tender. Discard bay leaf. Adjust seasoning to taste.

Serves 4-6

Shane met his wife Darleena when they were both attending grade school in Los Angeles. After being best friends throughout high school, they married and are now the proud parents of Shane Mack, Jr. Shane and Darleena like to travel, watch movies and spend time with family and friends. Fishing and bowling are favorite hobbies. Shane's secret wish? To be either a professional basketball player or a popular singer.

24 Outfielder

It's Outta Here! Chicken Chili

from Darleena and Shane Mack

LINE UP

6-8 boneless, skinless chicken
   breasts
1 28-ounce can whole tomatoes
1 32-ounce can kidney beans
1 clove garlic, minced
1 onion, sliced

1 cup frozen corn
½ green pepper, chopped
2 ribs celery, chopped
1 carrot, grated
2 teaspoons orange zest
salt and pepper to taste

PLAY-BY-PLAY

1. Place chicken and tomatoes in crock pot. Cook for 1 hour, until chicken falls to pieces.

2. Add all remaining ingredients, season to taste with salt and pepper. Simmer for 1½ hours. Serve with warm tortillas.

Serves 6-8

Chicken That Makes Its Own Gravy

from Marge and Jim Wiesner

LINE UP

¼ cup melted butter
2½ pounds chicken pieces
¼ cup flour
salt and pepper to taste
⅔ cup evaporated milk

1 can cream of mushroom soup
1 cup grated American cheese
1 small onion, chopped
4 mushrooms, chopped
paprika

PLAY-BY-PLAY

1. Preheat oven to 425 degrees. Pour melted butter into 9-by-13-inch baking pan.

2. Coat chicken in flour mixed with salt and pepper. Arrange skin down in baking dish. Bake for 45 minutes. Turn chicken and bake additional 15 minutes.

3. Combine milk, soup and cheese. Add onions and mushrooms and pour over chicken. Sprinkle with paprika. Cover pan with foil and bake for 20 minutes longer.

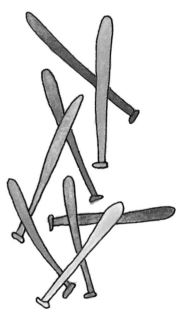

Serves 4

Pay-Off Pitch Parmesan Chicken

from Lisa Limbaugh and Eddie Guardado

LINE UP

2 cups Ritz cracker crumbs
½ cup grated sharp cheddar
cheese
1 cup grated parmesan cheese

2 tablespoons garlic salt
4 tablespoons corn oil
6 skinless, boneless chicken
breasts

PLAY-BY-PLAY

1. Preheat oven to 350 degrees. Lightly grease 9-by-13-inch glass baking dish.

2. Combine cracker crumbs, cheeses and garlic salt.

3. Dip chicken into corn oil, then roll in cracker mixture. Arrange in dish. Cover and bake for 1 hour.

Serves 6

After knowing each other for years, it wasn't until Eddie and his fiancée Lisa were partners in his brother's wedding that their romance really took off. Now they've set their own wedding date. Together they enjoy fishing, watching movies, taking long drives and "just being together." Eddie's hobbies include basketball and karate. The greatest day of his life was on June 8, 1993, when he was called up to the majors. If he wasn't playing baseball, he'd want to continue his career in criminal justice. Secret desire? "To live off the land in the woods, hunting, fishing and being away from civilization."

18 Pitcher

Pennant Chase Paprika Chicken

from Judi and Chip Hale

LINE UP

1 teaspoon salt
½ teaspoon pepper
1 cup flour
4 boneless, skinless
    chicken breasts

3 tablespoons olive oil
1 large onion, sliced
2 tablespoons sweet paprika
¼ cup water
1 cup sour cream

> ❝ This is
> one of Chip's
> favorites! ❞
>
> —Judi Hale

PLAY-BY-PLAY

1. Combine salt, pepper and flour. Dredge chicken breasts in seasoned flour. Shake off excess.

2. Heat oil in large sauté pan. Brown chicken 5 minutes each side. Remove from pan.

3. Add onions to sauté and brown. Stir in paprika.

4. Return chicken to sauté. Add water and simmer. When heated through, add sour cream. Heat 2 minutes.

Serves 4

Cheddar Chicken Risotto

from Sue and Terry Jorgensen

LINE UP

1 onion, chopped
2 tablespoons butter
4 ounces mushrooms, sliced
1½ cups rice
3 cups chicken broth, heated
*   to boiling*

1 pound boneless, skinless
*   chicken breasts, broiled and*
*   cut into thin strips*
1 cup shredded cheddar cheese

PLAY-BY-PLAY

1. In large saucepan, brown onion in butter. Add mushrooms, cook until tender. Add rice and cook for 4 minutes.

2. Stir hot chicken broth into vegetables and rice. Bring to a boil, cover and simmer until broth is almost gone, 15 minutes.

3. Gently stir in chicken, simmering until heated through and rice is tender. Stir in cheese and serve immediately.

Serves 6

Slugger's Sautéed Chicken

from Monica and David McCarty

> ❝ Use your choice of spices. I use all those listed here. …Dark meat works better for this sauté, white meat tends to dry out. ❞
>
> —Monica McCarty

LINE UP

2 tablespoons olive oil
1 pound boneless, skinless
    chicken, cut into 1½-inch
    pieces and patted dry
1 small onion, chopped
4 cloves garlic, crushed
2 ribs celery, chopped
6 mushrooms, sliced

1 zucchini, sliced
your favorite herbs, to taste:
    try parsley, dill, oregano
    and basil
crushed red pepper, to taste
¼ cup dry white wine
2 tablespoons grated parmesan
    cheese

PLAY-BY-PLAY

1. Heat olive oil in large sauté pan and add chicken, onion, garlic, celery, mushrooms and zucchini. Cook, stirring often, until chicken is brown, 5-10 minutes. Pour off fat.

2. Add herbs, red pepper and wine. Cook slowly over low heat for 10 minutes, until chicken is done. Remove to serving dish, sprinkle on parmesan, and serve.

Serves 4-6

Twig's Spiced Chicken

from Lin and Wayne Terwilliger

Lin, Wayne, and "Kat"

LINE UP

8-10 chicken pieces
2 bay leaves
salt and pepper to taste
6 ounces shell macaroni
2 tablespoons butter or
*   margarine*
1 small onion, chopped
2 tablespoons chili powder
2 tablespoons Worcestershire
*   sauce*
1 tablespoon plus 1½ teaspoons
*   mustard*
1 cup ketchup or tomato paste
1½ cups water

PLAY-BY-PLAY

1. Simmer chicken with bay leaves, salt and pepper, to desired doneness, begin checking after 25 minutes. Remove chicken from water.

2. Boil macaroni in the same water. Cook until done, about 10 minutes. Drain.

3. In large saucepan, melt butter and sauté onion until tender. Add chili powder, Worcestershire sauce, mustard, ketchup, water and salt and pepper to taste. Mix well, cook until slightly thickened.

4. Place macaroni in large serving dish and arrange chicken on top. Pour thickened sauce over all and serve.

Serves 6

Chicken Tetrazzini

from Jana and Jeff Reboulet

LINE UP

1 8-ounce can sliced mushrooms
⅓ cup margarine
4 boneless, skinless chicken
    breasts, cooked and cut into
    1½-inch pieces

8 ounces spaghetti, broken,
    cooked and drained
2 cans cream of chicken soup
2 cups sour cream
½ cup parmesan cheese

PLAY-BY-PLAY

1. Preheat oven to 300 degrees. Grease 9-by-13-inch glass baking dish.

2. Sauté mushrooms in margarine. Remove to large bowl.

3. Add chicken, spaghetti, soup and sour cream to sautéed mushrooms. Mix well and place in baking dish. Sprinkle parmesan over top. Bake for 40 minutes.

Serves 4

Basehit Breakfast Bake

from Robin and Lenny Webster

If using pork sausage, brown and drain first. Turkey sausage does not have to be pre-cooked.

LINE UP

*1 can refrigerator crescent
    dinner rolls*
½ pound pork or turkey sausage
*8 ounces shredded cheddar
    cheese*

5 eggs
¼ cup milk
*8 ounces shredded mozzarella
    cheese*

PLAY-BY-PLAY

1. Preheat oven to 350 degrees. Lightly grease 9-inch square baking pan.

2. Spread dinner rolls in bottom of pan, dot with sausage. Sprinkle cheddar cheese over sausage.

3. Combine eggs and milk and pour over cheddar cheese. Sprinkle mozzarella over all.

4. Bake for 30 minutes.

Serves 4

Batter Up Breakfast Crepes

from Danielle and Derek Parks

LINE UP

½ cup flour
½ cup milk
1 egg
1 tablespoon melted butter
   or margarine

1 tablespoon sugar
dash salt
filling — fruit, jam or butter
   and cinnamon sugar
whipped cream

*Danielle,
Homecoming Princess,
1982*

PLAY-BY-PLAY

1. Mix all ingredients except filling and whipped cream together until well blended. Let stand at room temperature for 1 hour.

2. Preheat large flat non-stick pan. Use a few drops of vegetable oil if necessary.

3. Pour one-third of batter into hot pan, swirling it to spread batter thin. When top bubbles, turn crepe. Cook briefly, then remove to large platter and keep warm while other crepes are cooking.

4. Fill crepes with fruit, jam, or butter and cinnamon sugar. Roll up and serve topped with whipped cream.

Makes 3 crepes

Derek and Danielle Parks "grew up together with baseball," having known each other since the Little League days. "Never in my wildest dreams did I ever think I would marry one of my little brother's closest friends," says Danielle. But they were married in 1987 and now have two beautiful daughters, Ashley and Chelsea. Derek and Danielle enjoy going to Lake Mojave for "water-skiing, heat and sunshine." They hope someday to travel to Australia. "We like to spend time getting together with friends, taking weekend trips with our families and settling down as full-time Mom and Dad to our kids. Our off-season is definitely family time."

16 **Catcher**

95

❝ Because we believe that there is a Divine plan for our lives, Brian has never had a 'good luck' dish. He does have some favorite dishes but none related to how well he does on the field. He is, however, aware of what he eats and is what one would consider health conscious. ❞

—Chris Harper

Chili Egg Puff

from Chris and Brian Harper

This dish is always a favorite with guests, and Brian loves it. I suggest fresh fruit and croissants to complete the meal.

LINE UP

10 eggs
½ cup flour
1 teaspoon baking powder
½ teaspoon salt

1 pound grated Monterey Jack cheese
1 pound creamed cottage cheese
½ cup melted butter
1 4½-ounce can diced chiles

PLAY-BY-PLAY

1. Preheat oven to 350 degrees. Grease 9-by-13-inch glass baking dish.

2. Beat eggs thoroughly. Add flour, baking powder, salt, cheeses and butter. Mix until smooth. Add chiles.

3. Pour batter into baking dish and bake for 35 minutes.

Serves 6-8 women or 4-6 hungry men!

Country Brunch

from Andrea and Mark Guthrie

LINE UP

9 slices white bread, crusts removed and cut into
 ½-inch squares
12 eggs, well beaten
4 tablespoons butter, cubed fine
3 cups milk
6 green onions, chopped
¼ cup chopped green pepper
¼ cup chopped red pepper
2 pounds pork sausage, browned, drained and crumbled
2 cups grated cheddar cheese
1 teaspoon salt
¼ teaspoon freshly ground pepper

❝ Great dish
for brunch—
all preparation
is done the
night before. ❞

—Andrea Guthrie

PLAY-BY-PLAY

1. Grease 9-by-13-inch glass baking dish.

2. Combine all ingredients and mix well. Pour into dish, cover
and refrigerate overnight.

3. Preheat oven to 300 degrees. Uncover dish and bake for
1 hour. Serve immediately.

Serves 12-14

Monterey, Mushroom and Egg Bake

from Jeanie and Kent Hrbek

❝ The only time I remember coming home to a fully cooked dinner was on our six month anniversary. Kent had made me beef stroganoff. I was pretty impressed! ❞

—Jeanie Hrbek

You can also add red or green pepper, shallots, and sausage to this do-ahead bake. Just sauté additional ingredients with the mushrooms and layer them under the cheeses.

LINE UP

1 1-pound loaf french bread, heels removed and torn into chunks
2 cups shredded Monterey Jack cheese
2 cups shredded cheddar cheese
8 ounces cream cheese, cubed

8 ounces mushrooms, sliced and sautéed in 2 tablespoons butter
10 eggs
2 cups milk
½ teaspoon dry mustard
dash cayenne pepper

PLAY-BY-PLAY

1. Grease 9-by-13-inch baking pan. Arrange bread evenly in pan and sprinkle with cheeses. Top with mushrooms.

2. Lightly beat eggs in large mixing bowl. Stir in milk, mustard, and cayenne. Pour over cheeses. Cover and chill several hours or overnight.

3. Remove pan from refrigerator one hour before baking. Preheat oven to 350 degrees. Bake uncovered for 55-60 minutes, until knife inserted in center comes out clean. Remove from oven and let stand 10 minutes before serving.

Serves 8

Make-the-Call Quiche

from Kathy and Herb Carneal

LINE UP

½ cup melted butter
1½ cups milk
¼ teaspoon salt
dash pepper
3 large eggs

½ cup Bisquick baking mix
1 cup shredded Swiss cheese
½ cup bacon or ham, cut into
    small pieces

PLAY-BY-PLAY

1. Preheat oven to 350 degrees.

2. Combine melted butter, milk, salt, pepper, eggs and Bisquick. Beat for 2 minutes. Add cheese and ham. Mix well, then pour into quiche pan or pie plate. The pan will be full to rim.

3. Bake for 50-60 minutes, until golden. Let set for 10 minutes before cutting.

Serves 6-8

After meeting his bride-to-be on a blind date, Herb proposed to Kathy by giving her a diamond ring during the 7th inning stretch of a game between the AAA Springfield Cubs and the AAA Buffalo Bisons. He's been broadcasting Twins games on the radio for more than 30 years. The mountains of Virginia (Herb's home state) and North Carolina are favorite getaways. If he wasn't involved with baseball, Herb would "be a doctor so I could help others."

Broadcaster "Voice of the Minnesota Twins"

Finding turnips in Minnesota that satisfy Gene's cravings seems to be "Mission Impossible" for Kathleen. She explains, "Gene's favorite food at holiday time is turnips — he grew up having them each and every Thanksgiving and Christmas. I've tried to buy them for him here in Minnesota, but to no avail. They just don't seem to taste quite like his mom's 'New York Style' turnips."

Impossible Vegetable Pie

from Kathleen and Gene Larkin

LINE UP

2 cups chopped broccoli steamed
    until tender (if using frozen,
    just thaw and drain)
½ cup chopped onion
½ cup chopped green pepper
1 cup shredded cheddar cheese

1½ cups milk
¾ cup Bisquick baking mix
3 eggs
1 teaspoon salt
¼ teaspoon pepper

PLAY-BY-PLAY

1. Preheat oven to 400 degrees. Lightly grease 9-inch pie plate.

2. Combine broccoli, onion, green pepper and cheese in pie plate. Beat milk, Bisquick, eggs, salt and pepper until smooth, pour over vegetables.

3. Bake pie until golden brown and knife inserted in center comes out clean, 35-40 minutes.

4. Remove pie from oven and let stand for 5 minutes before cutting.

Serves 6

All-Star Fried Catfish Fillet

from Tonya and Kirby Puckett

Goes great with baked potatoes and steamed vegetables.

LINE UP

5 fresh catfish fillets	*self-sealing plastic bag*
1 cup yellow cornmeal	*1 cup vegetable oil*
1 tablespoon Nature's Seasoning	*¼ cup margarine*

PLAY-BY-PLAY

1. Rinse fillets, blot dry with paper towel.

2. Shake cornmeal and seasoning together in self-sealing plastic bag. Add fillets, one at a time, shaking well to coat.

3. Heat oil and margarine in large skillet over medium heat. Add fillets, frying until golden brown on each side.

Serves 5

Tonya's favorite color is red and Kirby's favorite color is pink. When it comes to movies, just serve Kirby a big helping of "A Few Good Men" or "Scarface," two of his favorite films.

Fish Meuniere

from Tonya and Dave Winfield

❝ The only two foods that David and I shy away from are brussels sprouts and cauliflower. Other than that, we will eat just about any type of food and love to experiment with different ethnic foods. ❞

—Tonya Winfield

LINE UP

¼ cup lowfat milk
1 egg
⅓ cup flour
½ teaspoon salt
½ teaspoon cayenne pepper
4 fillets sole, catfish or bass
2 teaspoons vegetable oil

1 tablespoon butter or
   margarine
2 tablespoons lemon juice
2 tablespoons chopped fresh
   parsley
½ teaspoon Worcestershire sauce
parsley sprigs and lemon wedges

PLAY-BY-PLAY

1. In a shallow bowl, combine milk and egg. In another shallow bowl, combine flour, salt, and cayenne. Dip fillets first in milk mixture, then flour mixture. Shake off excess.

2. Heat oil in large non-stick sauté pan over medium heat. Add fillets and cook until golden brown, turning only once, 2-3 minutes per side. Fish should be opaque. Transfer fish to serving platter.

3. Meanwhile melt butter in a small saucepan. Stir in lemon juice, parsley and Worcestershire sauce. Spoon butter sauce over fish, garnish with parsley sprigs and lemon wedges, and serve.

Serves 4

Flyball Fisher's Feast

from Sue and Terry Jorgensen

LINE UP

3 ripe tomatoes, peeled and
    chopped
1 onion, sliced
1 green pepper, sliced
1 teaspoon olive oil

salt and pepper to taste
1 16-ounce can tomato sauce
1 pound red snapper, broiled
    and cut into strips
3 cups cooked rice

A recipe from family friends, Charles and Diana Fisher, of Portland, Oregon.

PLAY-BY-PLAY

1. Simmer tomatoes in their juices in a large saucepan for
30 minutes, adding water when necessary. In a separate pan, sauté
onion and pepper slices in oil. Season to taste with salt and pepper.

2. Add sautéed vegetables and tomato sauce to cooked tomatoes.
When heated through, add red snapper. Heat and mix well. Serve
over rice.

Serves 4

Fish with Onion and Pepper Rings

from Diane and Dick Martin

LINE UP

2 pounds fish fillets (trout,
    orange roughy, sierra)
juice and zest of 1 lemon
    (see tip, page 128)
3 tablespoons margarine
1 large clove garlic, minced
1 green pepper, seeded and sliced
    into thin rings

1 large onion, sliced into
    thin rings
¼ teaspoon salt
½ teaspoon pepper
½ cup white wine or
    chicken broth

PLAY-BY-PLAY

1. Arrange raw fish in a single layer on large platter. Sprinkle with lemon juice and zest and set aside.

2. Melt margarine in large sauté pan. Cook garlic, pepper and onion until tender. Do not over-brown. Remove with slotted spoon.

3. Raise heat to high and fry fish for 10 minutes. Turn fish and place onions and peppers on top. Sprinkle with salt and pepper if desired.

4. Cook fish for 10 minutes longer, adding more margarine if necessary. Fish should be golden and flaky. Remove to a heated serving platter, covering fish with vegetables.

5. Pour wine or broth into hot pan and heat for 2 minutes, scraping up browned bits. Pour sauce over fish and vegetables and serve.

Serves 4

French Fish Family Favorite

from Chris and Brian Harper

LINE UP

2 pounds orange roughy or other white fish
¾ cup chopped green onion
1 rib celery, chopped
¾ cup sliced mushrooms

1 cup white wine
1 can cream of mushroom soup
1¼ cups shredded cheddar cheese

PLAY-BY-PLAY

1. Preheat oven to 350 degrees. Spray 9-by-13-inch glass casserole with non-stick cooking spray.

2. Place fish on bottom of casserole. Layer onion, celery and mushrooms over fish. Combine wine and soup, pour over vegetables. Cover all with shredded cheese.

3. Bake for 40 minutes. Arrange fish on serving plates and spoon sauce over.

Serves 4

❝ I double this recipe for my family. This is the first fish dish that I ever liked. I have never been a seafood person, but this recipe changed me. For all you non-seafood people—give this a try, you will not be disappointed. ❞

—Chris Harper

Brian and Chris Harper were married in 1980 and have since moved 55 times! Yet they say, "We are living our dream." Natives of Los Angeles, Brian and Chris met at a dance when they were just 15 years old. Today they focus on their three boys, Brett, Derek and Lance, baseball and their faith in Jesus Christ. Says Chris, "A day does not pass where I am not reminded of God's grace toward us in giving Brian a career where we can enjoy wonderful foods and have the freedom to choose whatever we want to eat. Many, many people don't have this awesome privilege."

12 Catcher

No. 3's
Orange Roughy Waazoo

from Nita and Harmon Killebrew

Harmon Killebrew's number was formally retired by the Twins on August 11, 1974. One of the greatest home run hitters of all time, "Killer" was a member of the Twins from their inaugural season in 1961. He was elected to the Baseball Hall of Fame on January 10, 1984, the first Twin to receive that honor.

You can use swordfish, halibut, cod, dover sole or scrod for orange roughy.

LINE UP

4 cups cooked rice
3 tablespoons butter
1 tablespoon plus 1 teaspoon
   lemon juice
2 cans cream of salmon soup
1 can cream of celery soup
½ cup half and half

8 orange roughy fillets
¼ teaspoon pepper
½ teaspoon lemon pepper
½ teaspoon salt
2 tablespoons chopped parsley
lemon slices

PLAY-BY-PLAY

1. Preheat oven to 375 degrees. Spoon rice into 2½-quart casserole with cover.

2. Melt butter and add lemon juice, soups and half and half. Mix until smooth and heated thoroughly.

3. Arrange fish over rice in casserole and sprinkle with peppers and salt. Spoon soup mixture over, then sprinkle with parsley. Bake covered for 15 minutes, until fish is flaky. Serve garnished with lemon slices.

Serves 8

Sherry Sauced Shrimp

from Gordette and Tony Oliva

LINE UP

1 tablespoon olive oil
1 onion, chopped
2 cloves garlic, crushed and
    chopped
1 15-ounce can tomato sauce
¾ cup sherry

1½ teaspoons oregano
1 bay leaf
½ teaspoon salt
1 pound shrimp, peeled and
    deveined

PLAY-BY-PLAY

1. Heat olive oil in large sauté pan. Add onion and garlic and sauté until tender.

2. Add tomato sauce, sherry, basil, bay leaf and salt to sauté. Simmer for 30 minutes.

3. Add shrimp to sauté. Cook another 15 minutes until shrimp is done.

Serves 4

Pedro "Tony" Oliva is the only player to win American League batting titles in his first two seasons. The 1964 Rookie of the Year, "Tony O" retired with a .304 career average. He began his coaching career with the club in 1976. His number was formally retired on July 14, 1991.

Shrimp Scampi

from Karen and Mike Pagliarulo

LINE UP

¼ cup butter
½ cup oil
1 large onion, diced
4 cloves garlic, crushed and
    minced

1 pound shrimp, peeled and
    deveined
¼ cup bread crumbs
¼ cup chopped parsley
1 pound cooked linguini

> **❝ I can't cook without garlic. ❞**
>
> —Karen Pagliarulo

PLAY-BY-PLAY

1. Heat butter and oil in large sauté pan. Add onion and garlic, sauté, but do not brown.

2. Add shrimp to sauté and cook, turning when pink, about 5 minutes.

3. Sprinkle bread crumbs and parsley over shrimp and turn again. Cook 1 more minute until done, then serve over linguini.

Serves 5

For tips on crushing garlic, see the recipe for Tony O's Black Beans on page 154.

Base-Balsamic Swordfish

from Mary Ann and Jim Kaat

"What a Kaatch!"

❝ Fast, easy and healthy. ❞

—Jim Kaat

LINE UP

2 tablespoons balsamic vinegar
¼ cup chopped fresh cilantro
3 cloves garlic, crushed

10 ounces swordfish fillets
self-sealing plastic bag

PLAY-BY-PLAY

1. Combine all ingredients in plastic bag. Seal and marinate in refrigerator for 30 minutes.

2. Preheat grill or broiler. Remove fillets from bag and cook approximately 10 minutes per inch of thickness, brushing with marinade.

Serves 2

Shoestring Catch Tuna

from Jeanie and Kent Hrbek

" Kent's favorite. "

—Jeanie Hrbek

The basis of white sauces and meat gravies, roux is made by delicately cooking equal parts of butter and flour. For white sauce, the roux is kept light in color and warm milk is carefully stirred in. Use low heat so the sauce does not brown, and whisk constantly so no lumps form. Brown your roux for dark sauces or gravies, and add meat stock, stirring constantly.

LINE UP

4 tablespoons butter
4 tablespoons flour
½ teaspoon salt
½ teaspoon pepper
2 cups milk
2 cups diced celery, simmered until tender

2 6¼-ounce cans tuna, drained
2 tablespoons grated parmesan cheese
1 can cream of mushroom soup
1 cup shoestring potatoes

PLAY-BY-PLAY

1. Melt butter in medium saucepan over low heat. Blend in flour, salt and pepper. Stir until smooth and bubbly. Gradually add milk and bring to boil, stirring constantly until thickened.

2. Combine cooked celery, tuna, parmesan, and mushroom soup with white sauce. Cook until heated through. Serve on top of shoestring potatoes.

Serves 6

Can't Miss Angel Hair Pasta

from Monica and David McCarty

Great with sourdough bread. This quick and easy recipe also serves 6 as a side dish. For variety, you can add mushrooms or shrimp with tomatoes, or use shallots in place of garlic.

LINE UP

2-4 tablespoons olive oil
3 cloves garlic, mashed
6 ounces angel hair pasta
8 roma tomatoes, seeded and chopped

3 tablespoons finely chopped fresh basil
2 tablespoons parmesan cheese

> " It is a game to be savored rather than taken in gulps. "
>
> —Bill Veeck

PLAY-BY-PLAY

1. Heat 2 tablespoons olive oil in medium saucepan. Lightly brown garlic in oil. Turn heat to very low. Watch garlic so it doesn't burn.

2. Meanwhile, cook pasta in large pot of boiling water. About one minute before pasta is done, add tomatoes and basil to garlic and olive oil. Raise heat to medium and stir well to mix ingredients.

3. Drain pasta and toss with tomato mixture. Add more olive oil to taste. Serve sprinkled with parmesan cheese.

Serves 2

Joy's Chicken

from Andrea and Mark Guthrie

LINE UP

2 cloves garlic, minced
¼ cup extra virgin olive oil
¾ pound boneless, skinless
   chicken breast, cut into
   strips
2 cups broccoli florets
¾ cup oil-packed sun-dried
   tomatoes, drained and
   sliced thin

1 teaspoon dried basil
pinch red pepper flakes
salt and pepper to taste
¼ cup white wine
¾ cup chicken broth
1 tablespoon butter
12 ounces bow-tie pasta, cooked
   and drained
parmesan cheese

Recipe can be doubled.

PLAY-BY-PLAY

1. Sauté garlic in olive oil. Add chicken and sauté until cooked through.

2. Push chicken to one side and add broccoli, sautéing until crisp-tender. Add tomatoes, seasonings, wine and broth. Mix well. Add butter, cover and simmer for 5 minutes over low heat.

3. Remove from heat. Add pasta and toss. Serve with parmesan cheese.

Serves 4

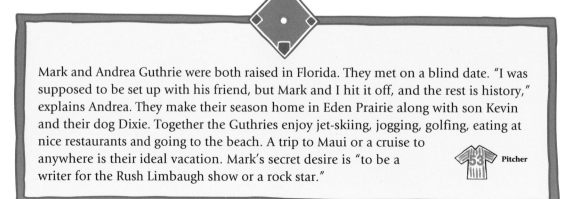

Mark and Andrea Guthrie were both raised in Florida. They met on a blind date. "I was supposed to be set up with his friend, but Mark and I hit it off, and the rest is history," explains Andrea. They make their season home in Eden Prairie along with son Kevin and their dog Dixie. Together the Guthries enjoy jet-skiing, jogging, golfing, eating at nice restaurants and going to the beach. A trip to Maui or a cruise to anywhere is their ideal vacation. Mark's secret desire is "to be a writer for the Rush Limbaugh show or a rock star."

Pitcher

Fastball Fettucine

from Barbara and Mike Trombley

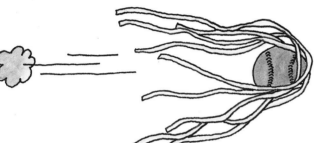

LINE UP

1 pound fettucine
12 ounces boneless, skinless
    chicken breast
1 tablespoon olive oil
pepper to taste
1 clove garlic, crushed and
    minced
1 bunch broccoli, cut into
    bite-sized pieces

2 tablespoons margarine
2 tablespoons flour
1½ teaspoons chicken bouillon
1 teaspoon salt
2½ cups milk
½ cup freshly grated parmesan
    cheese, plus more for
    garnishing
¼ cup toasted pine nuts

PLAY-BY-PLAY

1. Prepare fettucine. While pasta is cooking, sauté chicken in oil until fully cooked and juices run clear. Season to taste with pepper and garlic. Keep warm. Drain pasta when done.

2. Steam broccoli, covered, in 1 inch of boiling water until crisp-tender. Drain and keep warm.

3. Melt margarine over medium heat. Add flour, chicken bouillon and salt. Cook, stirring constantly for 1 minute. Gradually stir in milk. Heat and stir until mixture is smooth, thick and boiling. Boil for 1 minute longer. Remove sauce from heat and stir in cheese.

4. To serve, toss fettucine with chicken, broccoli and sauce. Top with pine nuts and serve with additional pepper and parmesan.

Serves 4-6

❝ This is one of my favorite recipes. We love alfredo sauce but find it very heavy. This sauce tastes similar, but is much lighter since it's made with milk. ❞

—Barbara Trombley

Texas Fettucine

from Lori and Jim Deshaies

With two jalapeños in the sauce, this pasta gets pretty hot. Remember to remove the veins and seeds before chopping the peppers. For milder flavor, use one 4½-ounce can of chopped green chiles in place of the jalapeños.

> ❝ My secret desire is to be in the studio audience of The Galloping Gourmet and be selected to taste the day's recipe. ❞
>
> —Jim Deshaies

LINE UP

3 boneless, skinless chicken breasts, cut into 1½-inch pieces
¼ cup olive oil
¼ cup white wine
1 cup chicken stock
¼ cup butter

4 ripe tomatoes, coarsely chopped
1 16-ounce can black beans, rinsed and drained
2 jalapeño peppers, chopped
½ cup chopped fresh cilantro
1 pound tri-color pasta, cooked and drained

PLAY-BY-PLAY

1. Brown chicken in hot oil. Deglaze pan with wine. Add chicken stock and boil for 15 minutes to reduce slightly. Add butter and cook for 3 minutes.

2. Add tomatoes and beans to chicken, heat through. Remove from heat. Stir in jalapeños and cilantro. Toss with pasta and serve.

Serves 4-6

Deglazing lifts off the browned bits of cooked food from your sauté pan, binding them with wine or broth to produce a thick and rich sauce for your dish. After sautéing meat, keep the pan very hot and throw in the wine or broth called for in the recipe. It will make a lot of noise, but will bubble down to a tasty sauce.

Leadoff Lasagna

from Monica and Bill Mahre

LINE UP

1 pound lean ground beef
6 ounces lean ground pork
1 onion, chopped
1 clove garlic, minced
1 16-ounce can tomatoes
1 15-ounce can tomato sauce
3 tablespoons parsley flakes
2 tablespoons sugar

1 teaspoon basil
3 cups small curd cottage cheese
1 cup grated parmesan cheese
1 teaspoon oregano
8 ounces lasagna noodles,
*   cooked and drained*
12 ounces mozzarella cheese,
*   shredded*

Freezes perfectly,
great for entertaining.

PLAY-BY-PLAY

1. Cook beef, pork, onion and garlic in large saucepan until meat is browned and onion is tender. Drain off fat. Add tomatoes, breaking up with fork. Stir in tomato sauce, 2 tablespoons of the parsley, sugar and basil. Heat to boiling, stirring occasionally. Reduce heat and simmer until thick, at least one hour.

2. Preheat oven to 350 degrees. Reserve ½ cup meat sauce and set aside. Combine cottage cheese, ½ cup parmesan, remaining tablespoon parsley and oregano, set aside.

3. Layer one fourth of the noodles in 9-by-13-inch baking pan. Top with one fourth each of the meat sauce, mozzarella cheese, and cottage cheese mixture. Repeat this arrangement three times.

4. Spread reserved meat sauce over top and sprinkle with remaining parmesan cheese. At this point, lasagna can be covered and refrigerated if desired for advance preparation.

5. Bake for 45-60 minutes. Allow extra 15 minutes if lasagna was refrigerated. Remove from oven and let stand 15 minutes before serving for easier cutting.

Serves 6-8

Mac 'n Cheese, Sure to Please

from Tonya and Dave Winfield

LINE UP

8 ounces macaroni, cooked and drained
8 ounces grated cheddar cheese
1 egg, beaten
2 cups evaporated milk
1 teaspoon salt
2 tablespoons butter or margarine

PLAY-BY-PLAY

1. Preheat oven to 350 degrees. Grease 2-quart casserole.

2. Layer half of the macaroni in the bottom of the casserole. Top with half of the cheese. Repeat layers.

3. Combine egg, milk and salt. Pour over the macaroni and cheese. Dot with butter and bake for 40 minutes.

Serves 2, or 4-6 as a side dish

Major League Manicotti

from Jana and Jeff Reboulet

Be sure to try this recipe. You'll be able to clean up as you go, even with a 5-year-old chasing you around the kitchen. Just don't let the manicotti shells get too soft, or they'll be hard to stuff.

LINE UP

1 tablespoon olive oil
1 pound ground beef
1 small onion, chopped
1 egg, slightly beaten
¼ cup grated Romano cheese
¼ cup seasoned bread crumbs

1 tablespoon chopped parsley
salt and pepper to taste
8 manicotti shells, cooked
*   until tender*
1½ pounds spaghetti sauce

> **❝ Baseball is the greatest of American games. ❞**
>
> —Thomas Edison

PLAY-BY-PLAY

1. Preheat oven to 350 degrees.

2. Heat olive oil and sauté beef and onion until beef is brown and onion is tender. Remove to mixing bowl.

3. Add egg, cheese, bread crumbs and parsley to beef and mix well. Season with salt and pepper.

4. Cover bottom of 9-by-13-inch baking dish with half of the spaghetti sauce. Fill manicotti shells with beef mixture and place on top of sauce in dish. Cover with remaining sauce.

5. Bake for 20 minutes.

Serves 4

Pag's Pasta Fagoli

from Karen and Mike Pagliarulo

❝ This recipe is always good for a three- or four-hit game! ❞

—Karen Pagliarulo

If you are not serving immediately, remove most of the sauce from the pasta when the pasta is still chewy, and store separately. Otherwise, the pasta will swell and soak up all the sauce.

LINE UP

1 pound chili mac macaroni
1 tablespoon olive oil
1 clove garlic, chopped
1 6-ounce can tomato paste

salt, pepper, crushed red pepper
 and basil to taste
1 cup grated Romano cheese
1 16-ounce can white beans,
 rinsed and drained

PLAY-BY-PLAY

1. Begin to cook pasta in salted boiling water to cover by 2 inches. Meanwhile, heat oil in sauté pan, add garlic and cook lightly. Add tomato paste, salt, pepper and red pepper to taste.

2. When pasta is still hard, add tomato mixture to boiling water. Sprinkle in cheese and basil to taste. Add beans. Cook until pasta is done, and sauce is thickened.

Serves 4-6

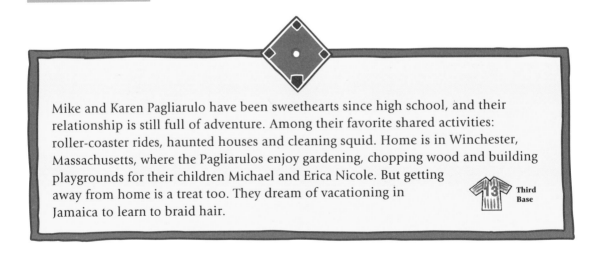

Mike and Karen Pagliarulo have been sweethearts since high school, and their relationship is still full of adventure. Among their favorite shared activities: roller-coaster rides, haunted houses and cleaning squid. Home is in Winchester, Massachusetts, where the Pagliarulos enjoy gardening, chopping wood and building playgrounds for their children Michael and Erica Nicole. But getting away from home is a treat too. They dream of vacationing in Jamaica to learn to braid hair.

13 **Third Base**

Bleacher Seat Black Olive Pasta

from Andrea and Mark Guthrie

LINE UP

1 tablespoon olive oil
1 clove garlic, chopped fine
1 small onion, chopped
1 16-ounce can salt-free whole
 tomatoes
1 cup pitted black olives, broken
 or coarsely chopped

3 tablespoon capers, rinsed and
 drained
1 tablespoon balsamic vinegar
2 tablespoons tomato paste
2 teaspoons sugar
1½ teaspoons oregano
1 pound cooked pasta

PLAY-BY-PLAY

1. Heat olive oil in large sauté pan over medium heat. Add garlic and onion and cook until tender.

2. Add tomatoes, breaking them up with wooden spoon. Stir in olives, capers, vinegar, tomato paste, sugar and oregano.

3. Simmer 10 minutes, until slightly thick. Serve over cooked pasta.

Serves 4-6

Balsamic vinegar is so full-flavored because it is made from grape juices that have been reduced to a sweet syrup, but not allowed to ferment. Balsamic vinegar is aged in oak and fruit wood casks, sometimes those used for spirits, for more than 50 years. It perks up the flavors in vegetable and bean dishes. The Italians even douse fresh strawberries with balsamic vinegar!

Perfect Game Pasta

from Lin and Wayne Terwilliger

A very easy and quick recipe that's great for summer since the sauce needs no cooking!

LINE UP

1 28-ounce can crushed
    tomatoes with added puree
2 tablespoons chopped fresh basil
handful sliced black olives
⅓ cup olive oil

3 cloves garlic, crushed
salt and pepper to taste
1 pound angel hair pasta
¼ cup parmesan cheese

PLAY-BY-PLAY

1. Combine tomatoes and puree, basil, black olives, olive oil, garlic and salt and pepper. Let stand 15 minutes.

2. Meanwhile, cook pasta and drain very well.

3. Toss sauce with pasta and divide between four plates. Sprinkle parmesan cheese over each and serve.

Serves 4

In 1972, a postman in Arlington, Texas set up a blind date for Wayne, his neighbor, and Lin, who worked as an artist and writer for a newspaper where he delivered mail. Two years later, "Twig" and Lin were married. They raised four children, Steve, Marcie, Mike and Kevin, and now enjoy three grandchildren. Fishing, playing cards and traveling are favorite pastimes of the Terwilligers, who make their home in Mound, Minnesota. Their dream getaway? "A secluded lake, a rustic cabin with a cozy fire and lots of fish!"

45 **First Base Coach**

Pasta Primavera

from Chris and Brian Harper

An incredible meal for a special occasion. This dish requires at least two hours of preparation time. It is worth every minute.

LINE UP

8 medium asparagus spears, ends snapped then peeled, cut diagonally into 1-inch pieces

3 zucchini, halved lengthwise, seeded, cut into 1-inch moons

3 yellow summer squash, cut into rounds

3 carrots, peeled and diced

1 head cauliflower, separated into florets

1 bunch broccoli, separated into florets

1 clove garlic, pressed or minced

salt and pepper to taste

2½ cups freshly grated parmesan cheese, plus more to taste

3½ cups heavy cream

5 egg yolks

2 tablespoons butter

10 mushrooms, sliced

3 large tomatoes, peeled, seeded and chopped

2 pounds cooked pasta, such as fettucine

PLAY-BY-PLAY

1. In boiling salted water, separately blanch all vegetables except mushrooms and tomatoes until just tender. Drain each vegetable and run under cold water to stop cooking.

2. In a large sauté pan, combine garlic, salt and pepper, 2½ cups parmesan, cream and egg yolks. Mix well and heat over a low flame to almost boiling.

3. Meanwhile, in small pan melt butter and sauté mushrooms for 2 minutes. Add with tomatoes and blanched vegetables to cream sauce. Mix well.

4. Combine pasta and sauce. Serve immediately on warm plates, passing additional parmesan cheese.

Serves 6-8

Vegetables can be blanched in advance to ease preparation. Rinse asparagus and bend each spear near the base. The end will snap off; discard it. If you wish, you may thinly peel 2 inches of the base end of each spear. To peel tomatoes, plunge in boiling water for 1 minute. Drain, cut through the peel and slip it off.

Jeanie's Stuffed Shells

from Jeanie and Kent Hrbek

When Kent cooked dinner for me on our six month anniversary, he told me he took the recipe out of my recipe box, went to the store and handed it to the clerk and told her he needed everything on the card! Although someone else did the shopping, it was still a delicious, memorable meal.

—Jeanie Hrbek

LINE UP

10 ounces frozen spinach, cooked and drained well
1 cup ricotta cheese
10 ounces shredded mozzarella cheese
½ cup grated parmesan cheese plus more to taste
3 eggs, beaten with fork
1 tablespoon plus 2 teaspoons melted margarine
1 tablespoon fennel seed

¼ teaspoon nutmeg
½ cup dried parsley
12 ounces jumbo shell pasta, cooked, drained and cooled
1 30-ounce jar chunky spaghetti sauce with tomatoes and mushrooms
1 8-ounce can tomato sauce
1 tablespoon plus 1 teaspoon sugar

PLAY-BY-PLAY

1. Preheat oven to 350 degrees. Grease 9-by-13-inch baking pan.

2. Combine spinach, cheeses, eggs, 2 teaspoons margarine, 1 teaspoon of the fennel seed, nutmeg and ¼ cup of the parsley. Fill each shell with 1 heaping teaspoon of cheese-spinach mixture. Arrange in baking pan.

3. Heat together spaghetti sauce, tomato sauce, sugar, remaining 1 tablespoon margarine, 2 teaspoons fennel seed, and ¼ cup parsley. Pour over shells. Sprinkle parmesan cheese over all and bake for 30 minutes.

Serves 8-10

Light Lasagna

from Barbara and Mike Trombley

Mike's mom Helene had the idea to use cottage cheese instead of ricotta in this lasagna recipe. It tastes the same and is lower in fat—it's great reheated so don't hesitate to make a full pan. We use Prego pasta sauce.

LINE UP

24 ounces cottage cheese
garlic salt, salt, pepper and
    oregano to taste
1 quart marinara pasta sauce
1 pound lasagna noodles, cooked

1 pound lean ground beef or
    turkey, browned and drained
4 ounces shredded mozzarella
½ cup parmesan cheese

PLAY-BY-PLAY

1. Preheat oven to 350 degrees. Season cottage cheese with garlic salt, salt, pepper and oregano.

2. Spread ¼ cup of the sauce in the bottom of 9-by-13-inch baking dish. Cover with a single layer of noodles. Spread meat evenly over noodle layer.

3. Spread ⅓ of remaining sauce over meat. Cover with another single layer of noodles. Spread seasoned cottage cheese over noodle layer and top with half of remaining sauce. Cover sauce with final single layer of noodles and spread remaining sauce over all.

4. Cover baking dish with aluminum foil and bake for 40 minutes. Remove foil and sprinkle lasagna with cheese, as desired. Bake for another 5 minutes. Remove from oven and let lasagna sit 10 minutes before cutting and serving.

Serves 9

To keep lasagna noodles from sticking together while you're assembling the dish, have the cooked noodles handy in a large pot of cold water. Drain the noodles one by one as you use them.

Crisp Roast Ducks on the Pond

from Diane and Dick Martin

LINE UP

1 teaspoon instant chicken
   bouillon
1 cup boiling water

2 1½-2-pound ducks
½ cup apple jelly
3 tablespoons apple juice

PLAY-BY-PLAY

1. Preheat oven to 375 degrees. Line roasting pan with foil. Dissolve bouillon in water.

2. Rinse ducks thoroughly and pat dry, inside and out. Place breast side up in pan.

3. Roast ducks for 1-2 hours, basting often with chicken bouillon mixture and pan drippings.

4. Combine apple jelly and apple juice in small saucepan. Heat until jelly melts.

5. Brush glaze on duck the last ten to fifteen minutes of roasting time. Cut ducks in half lengthwise to serve.

Serves 4

New Orleans Jambalaya

LINE UP

3 tablespoons butter or
    margarine
1 small clove garlic, minced
1 green pepper, chopped
1 small onion, chopped
5 pre-cooked pork sausages or
    1 cup chopped ham
1 16-ounce can whole tomatoes

1½ pounds raw cleaned shrimp,
    or 2½ cups diced cooked
    chicken
2 cups water
1 bay leaf
1 teaspoon salt
¼ teaspoon pepper
dash cayenne pepper
1 cup rice

PLAY-BY-PLAY

1. Melt butter in large saucepan over low heat. Sauté garlic and green pepper. Add onion and sausage or ham, sauté for 5 minutes.

2. Add tomatoes to saucepan, breaking up with spoon.
Add shrimp or chicken, water, bay leaf, salt, pepper and cayenne. Bring to a boil.

3. Stir in rice, lower heat to simmer. Cover and cook 30 minutes, until rice is fluffy.

Serves 6

❝ When we cook at home, it will often have a New Orleans flair. Because I am from the Crescent City, I was taught how to cook Creole and Cajun food by my mother, who is an excellent cook. ❞

—Tonya Winfield

Spiced Pork Tenderloin

from Rebecca and Robert Pohlad

LINE UP

1½ teaspoons sugar
1 teaspoon Kosher salt
1 teaspoon pepper
½ teaspoon coriander
¼ teaspoon cloves

2 12-ounce pork tenderloins,
   trimmed of fat
1 teaspoon olive oil
½ cup maple syrup

PLAY-BY-PLAY

1. Begin one day before serving: In a small bowl, combine sugar, salt, pepper, coriander and cloves.

2. Place the tenderloins in a shallow glass baking dish and rub the spice mixture into meat. Cover and refrigerate overnight.

3. Next day: Preheat grill. Brush each loin with olive oil and grill over moderate heat for 25 minutes, brushing 4-5 times with maple syrup. When done, internal temperature should be 155 degrees.

4. Remove from heat, let rest for 10 minutes. Brush meat again with syrup. Slice tenderloins across the grain into ¼-inch thick slices. To serve, arrange 7-8 slices in a fan on each plate.

Serves 4

MVP PBJ

from Tonya and Kirby Puckett

When Kirby was asked to give some examples of foods he favors for big games and winning streaks, he covered all the bases with a single answer: peanut butter and grape jelly sandwiches.

LINE UP

2 slices whole wheat bread
3 tablespoons Skippy peanut butter

2 tablespoons Welch's grape jelly
8 ounces 2% milk

> ❝ Always a winner! ❞
>
> —Tonya Winfield

PLAY-BY-PLAY

1. Spread peanut butter on one slice of wheat bread. Spread jelly over other slice.

2. Lay the slices gently together, with peanut butter and jelly facing each other.

3. Serve with an 8-ounce glass of 2% milk.

Serves 1

Raspberry Orange Turkey

from Sherry and Rick Aguilera

> ❝ I made this turkey for Rick and me on our first Christmas in Minnesota. It was also our first Christmas with our daughter Rachel, and away from our families (they all live in California). I set a fancy table in front of the fire and we had an elegant, cozy dinner *after* Rachel went to bed. ❞
>
> —Sherry Aguilera

LINE UP

1 2-pound turkey breast roast
1 cup orange juice
1 teaspoon ground sage
½ teaspoon thyme leaves
½ teaspoon pepper

½ teaspoon salt
1 teaspoon orange zest
2 cups raspberries, if frozen,
    do not thaw
⅓ cup sugar

PLAY-BY-PLAY

1. Preheat oven to 350 degrees.

2. Place turkey roast in shallow 9-by-9- or 7-by-11-inch baking pan. Pour orange juice over turkey, then sprinkle with sage, thyme, pepper, salt and orange zest.

3. Roast turkey for 1 hour and 20 minutes, basting with pan juices.

4. Combine raspberries and sugar. Place in baking pan around turkey roast. Continue roasting for 10-15 minutes. Remove from oven and let stand for 10 minutes before slicing.

Serves 8

Zest is the colored, outermost layer of a citrus peel. Use a grater to remove the zest from the peel. Be careful not to grate down to the pith (the white layer just underneath the zest). The zest adds aroma and essence while the pith is simply bitter.

Red Beans, Home Runs, and Rice

from Tonya and Kirby Puckett

" Goes great with corn muffins. "

—Tonya Puckett

LINE UP

1 pound dried red kidney beans
1 large ham shank
8 cups cold water

1 large onion
2 tablespoons plus 1½ teaspoons
*   Nature's Seasoning*
3 cups Minute Rice

PLAY-BY-PLAY

1. Rinse beans and soak in cool water to cover for 2 hours.

2. Rinse ham shank and put with water in crock pot to boil. Add onion and seasoning.

3. Drain beans and add to crock pot. Cook on low for 8-10 hours, until beans are soft. When done, fork should go through beans easily. Taste for seasoning.

4. Prepare the Minute Rice according to package directions and serve beans over.

Serves 6-8

You can substitute seasoned salt for the Nature's Seasoning. Or just add salt, pepper, onion, garlic, parsley, celery seed, and any other favorite spices to taste.

Kirby and Tonya Puckett are the perfect complement— he loves any sport except golf and she doesn't like any. Except, of course, baseball. They heartily agree on one thing, however, they love kids. They have two of their own, Catherine and Kirby Jr. And they've touched the lives of countless others through the Children's Heart Fund, where Kirby is a different kind of MVP. Together Kirby and Tonya enjoy traveling, going out to dinner, watching movies and "just spending quality time talking." If he weren't playing baseball, Kirby would like to be a police officer, and Tonya would like to be an actress. Something Kirby lives by: "Don't try to change things you have no control over."

34 Outfield

Dixie-Style Red Beans and Sausage

from Tonya and Dave Winfield

" We enjoy traveling all over the world. While traveling, David will always practice his photography. He loves this and has even had professional exhibits for some of his work. "

—Tonya Winfield

LINE UP

1 pound red or kidney beans
8 cups water
1 onion, chopped
4 cloves garlic, chopped
1 small green pepper, chopped

3 tablespoons chili powder
1 bay leaf
1 pound smoked beef sausage, diced, or 1 ham shank
4 cups steamed rice

PLAY-BY-PLAY

1. Rinse beans and soak in cold water to cover for one hour. Drain.

2. Cook 8 cups water, onion, garlic and pepper in large stock pot for 5 minutes. Add beans, chili powder, bay leaf and the ham shank, if using. Simmer on low heat for 30 minutes. Add half of the sausage and cook for another 30 minutes.

3. Remove 3 tablespoons of the beans and mash. Return them to the pot and stir. Add rest of sausage and continue cooking until bean gravy becomes thick and beans are soft. Serve over rice.

Serves 4-6

Dave and Tonya Winfield met in Los Angeles during the 1981 World Series. "When I first met David, I knew that he was the one for me. I wasn't sure if he would be my husband or my very best friend. He turned out to be both!" says Tonya. The Winfields especially enjoy traveling and "lean toward places with adventure." Their all-time favorite trip was an African safari. When it comes to food, Dave and Tonya enjoy eating out as much as they enjoy eating at home. "We just love to experiment with new restaurants and various cuisines. We eat just about any type of food and love to try different ethnic foods."

32 DH/Outfield

Hot Streak Pork Marinade

from Gordette and Tony Oliva

LINE UP

½ cup lemon juice
½ cup lime juice
1 onion, chopped
3 cloves garlic, crushed

1 tablespoon oregano
1 bay leaf
1 tablespoon vinegar
salt
2 pounds pork, pieces or roast

PLAY-BY-PLAY

1. Begin one day before serving: Combine all ingredients except pork in large glass bowl.

2. For pork pieces, add to bowl and stir to coat. For pork roast, place roast in a glass baking dish. With a small sharp knife, puncture holes all over roast and fill with marinade. Rub remaining marinade over outside of roast.

4. Refrigerate pork in marinade overnight.

5. Next day: Use your favorite method to cook the pork: grill, bake or fry until only very slightly pink inside. Pork dries out quickly, so watch closely.

Serves 4-6

❝ It always seemed as though my mother had so little in the cupboard but she served our family of 12 easily. We ate lots of rice, a variety of vegetables and many kinds of beans. A small amount of meat or chicken went a long way. ❞

—Tony Oliva

"As a young boy in Cuba, I always paid attention to how and what my mother cooked because I wanted to learn. Her dishes always tasted great. Living in the country, we grew and raised most of our own food." Today, Tony and Gordette still cook his mother's recipes, among other dishes. They love cooking together. Tony and Gordette make their home in Minneapolis, where they met when she came to town on her Senior Skip Day. Now they've been married more than 25 years and have three grown children, Anita, Pedro and Rick. Tony's outside interests include baseball, baseball and baseball.

6 Outfield/ DH

WHO'S WHO

See page 239

Short Stops
Salads and Sides

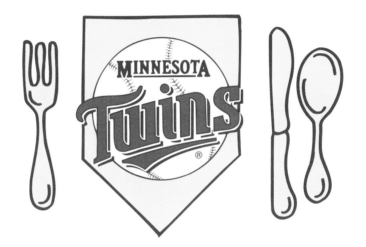

Short Stops
Salads and Sides

On Base Broccoli Salad

from Shannon and Kevin Mather

LINE UP

3 ounces bacon pieces
*2 bunches broccoli, cut
    into florets*
6 small green onions, chopped
2 cups chopped celery
½ cup slivered almonds

1 cup golden raisins
2 cups red grapes, halved
1 cup mayonnaise
1 tablespoon white vinegar
¼ cup sugar
¼ cup evaporated milk

PLAY-BY-PLAY

1. Make sure vegetables are very dry. Combine bacon, broccoli, onions, celery, almonds, raisins and grapes in serving bowl.

2. Mix together mayonnaise, vinegar, sugar and evaporated milk. Stir until sugar dissolves.

3. Immediately before serving, toss salad with dressing.

Serves 8

Brookville Coleslaw

from Cori and Pat Meares

Whipping the cream is the key to this delicious recipe.

LINE UP

4 cups chopped cabbage
⅓ cup sugar
½ teaspoon salt

2 tablespoons vinegar
½ cup heavy cream, whipped

PLAY-BY-PLAY

1. Combine all ingredients.
2. Place in serving bowl and refrigerate for 1 hour.

Serves 6

❝ This coleslaw originated at the famous Brookville Hotel in Brookville, Kansas. The Brookville opened in the 1800's and continues to be a popular old-fashioned, family-style inn and restaurant. ❞

—Cori Meares

Pat and Cori Meares began "going together" in seventh grade after having met at a school Halloween Fun Night. Pat's love of food dates back to his childhood, too. The Dr. Seuss classic, "Green Eggs and Ham" is one of his all-time favorite books. Today the Meares like to entertain at home, play golf and travel. A deserted beach in the Virgin Islands appeals to them. Pat's recipe for a successful game is "to eat well-balanced meals and get plenty of sleep. I also bought a troll doll for good luck." His secret desires? "To be a drummer, guitarist and lead singer for a rock band."

2 Shortstop

Caribbean Cruise, 1982

Sherry's Caesar Salad

from Sherry and Rick Aguilera

LINE UP

2 heads romaine lettuce
½ cup olive oil
3 cloves garlic
2 tablespoons lemon juice
4 anchovy fillets

salt and pepper to taste
2 tablespoons cold water
½ cup freshly grated parmesan
   cheese

PLAY-BY-PLAY

1. Wash and thoroughly dry all leaves. Cut lettuce into bite-sized pieces and place in serving bowl.

2. Combine olive oil and garlic in blender or food processor and blend until smooth and creamy. Add lemon juice and anchovies and blend. Season with salt and pepper. Add water, blend, and adjust seasoning to your taste.

3. Add only enough dressing to coat and glisten each piece of lettuce. Gently toss with hands, then sprinkle with parmesan and serve.

Serves 4-6

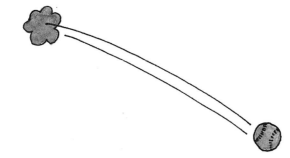

Swing for the Fences Salad

from Shannon and Kevin Mather

For the ultimate touch, freeze or chill the salad plates before you serve the salads.

LINE UP

3 tablespoons olive oil
2 tablespoons red wine vinegar
2 teaspoons lemon juice
1 teaspoon salt
½ teaspoon sugar
½ teaspoon oregano
¼ teaspoon pepper
2 cloves garlic, minced
½ head iceberg lettuce

½ head romaine lettuce
3 tomatoes, cut in wedges
½ cup shredded carrots
⅓ cup mild banana pepper rings
¼ cup parmesan cheese
1 red onion, chopped
1 cucumber, sliced
croutons

PLAY-BY-PLAY

1. Combine olive oil, vinegar, lemon juice, salt, sugar, oregano, pepper, and garlic in blender or food processor. Blend until smooth.

2. Combine lettuce and vegetables in large serving bowl. Toss with dressing. Serve with croutons.

Serves 6

Curveball Curry and Rice

from Judi and Chip Hale

LINE UP

6 ounces marinated artichoke
  hearts
4 ounces green olives, chopped
3 green onions, chopped
½ green or red pepper, chopped
1 cup cooked diced chicken

2¾ ounces slivered almonds
1 package chicken Rice-a-Roni,
  prepared and cooled
½ cup mayonnaise
1 teaspoon curry powder

PLAY-BY-PLAY

1. Drain artichoke hearts, reserving marinade for dressing.
Add artichokes, olives, onions, pepper, chicken and almonds to
cooled rice.

2. Combine reserved marinade with mayonnaise and curry powder.
Mix well. Stir dressing into rice salad until well mixed. Chill.

Serves 8

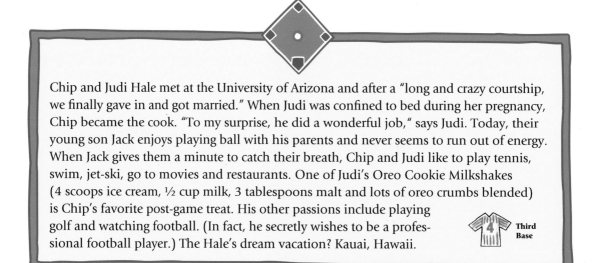

Chip and Judi Hale met at the University of Arizona and after a "long and crazy courtship,
we finally gave in and got married." When Judi was confined to bed during her pregnancy,
Chip became the cook. "To my surprise, he did a wonderful job," says Judi. Today, their
young son Jack enjoys playing ball with his parents and never seems to run out of energy.
When Jack gives them a minute to catch their breath, Chip and Judi like to play tennis,
swim, jet-ski, go to movies and restaurants. One of Judi's Oreo Cookie Milkshakes
(4 scoops ice cream, ½ cup milk, 3 tablespoons malt and lots of oreo crumbs blended)
is Chip's favorite post-game treat. His other passions include playing
golf and watching football. (In fact, he secretly wishes to be a professional football player.) The Hale's dream vacation? Kauai, Hawaii.

4 Third
Base

Best Chicken Salad Ever

from Nancy and John Gordon

LINE UP

1 8-ounce can pineapple chunks, drained and 2 tablespoons juice reserved
⅔ cup mayonnaise
1 tablespoon Dijon mustard
¾ teaspoon curry powder
dash salt
4 cups cooked chicken, cubed

¼ cup thinly sliced celery
2 tablespoons thinly sliced green onion
⅓ cup toasted slivered almonds
⅓ cup raisins
lettuce leaves
pineapple and grapes

PLAY-BY-PLAY

1. Combine 2 tablespoons pineapple juice, mayonnaise, mustard, curry powder and salt. Set aside.

2. Combine pineapple, chicken, celery, onion, almonds and raisins. Pour dressing over and mix well. Refrigerate at least 1 hour.

3. Serve on lettuce leaves, garnished with pineapple and grapes.

Serves 4

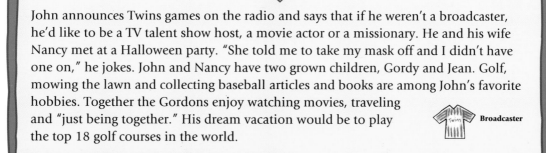

John announces Twins games on the radio and says that if he weren't a broadcaster, he'd like to be a TV talent show host, a movie actor or a missionary. He and his wife Nancy met at a Halloween party. "She told me to take my mask off and I didn't have one on," he jokes. John and Nancy have two grown children, Gordy and Jean. Golf, mowing the lawn and collecting baseball articles and books are among John's favorite hobbies. Together the Gordons enjoy watching movies, traveling and "just being together." His dream vacation would be to play the top 18 golf courses in the world.

Broadcaster

Thai-Ballgame Chicken Salad

from Sherry and Rick Aguilera

ff Rick likes this best if I double the dressing. JJ

—Sherry Aguilera

LINE UP

⅓ cup salad oil
2 tablespoons peanut butter
1 tablespoon plus 1 teaspoon
   soy sauce
1 tablespoon plus 1 teaspoon
   rice vinegar
1½ teaspoons sugar

1 tablespoon water
dash crushed red pepper
3 green onions, chopped
2 cups cooked chicken, cubed
lettuce leaves
1 cup bean sprouts
1 cucumber, sliced
½ cup peanuts

PLAY-BY-PLAY

1. In large bowl, whisk together oil, peanut butter, soy sauce, vinegar, sugar, water and red pepper. Stir in onions.

2. Add chicken pieces to dressing, toss to coat.

3. Serve salad on lettuce leaves, garnish with sprouts, cucumber and peanuts.

Serves 4

Rick, Sherry, and Rachel

Grab Bag Green Salad

from Jeanie and Kent Hrbek

LINE UP

1 cup olive oil
¼ cup white wine vinegar
¼ cup red wine vinegar
1 teaspoon salt
¼ teaspoon pepper
1 teaspoon Dijon mustard
¼ cup chopped parsley

2 cloves garlic, minced
8-gallon plastic bag
2 heads torn lettuce leaves
assorted salad vegetables
croutons, parmesan cheese
    to taste

PLAY-BY-PLAY

1. Combine oil, vinegars, salt, pepper, mustard, parsley and garlic in blender or food processor. Blend until smooth.

2. Combine lettuce leaves and salad vegetables in plastic bag. Add enough dressing to coat salad and shake well. Serve in large salad bowl.

Serves 12

❝ It's in the bag! This recipe is excellent entertainment for a crowd. Fill the bag with greens, and have each guest bring their favorite salad ingredient, such as black olives, croutons or parmesan cheese. We did this for our wine-tasting party and it was a hit! ❞

—Jeanie Hrbek

McCarty's Mandarin Orange Salad

from Monica and David McCarty

Monica recommends "Paul Newman's Own" Italian salad dressing to coat this fresh salad.

Take care of your knives. Keep them very sharp so you use the blade, not pressure, to cut. Cut fruits and vegetables in half first to create a flat side. Place flat side down on cutting surface to slice or chop without slipping.

LINE UP

1 large head romaine lettuce, rinsed, dried and ripped into bite-sized pieces

1 12-ounce can mandarin orange segments, drained

1 purple onion

1 large cucumber, peeled and sliced into bite-sized pieces

½ cup walnuts

8 ounces Italian salad dressing

PLAY-BY-PLAY

1. Combine lettuce and orange segments in large salad bowl.

2. Cut onion in half and slice off 10 very thin slices from each half. Separate onion segments and add to salad bowl.

3. Add cucumber and walnuts to salad. Toss with dressing to taste.

Serves 4-6

Taste Testing with "Turtle"

GM's Mexican Salad

from Lark and Andy MacPhail

LINE UP

1 purple onion
1 head iceberg lettuce
4 tomatoes
4 ounces grated cheddar cheese
8 ounces Thousand Island or
    French dressing to taste
dash of tabasco sauce
1 pound ground round

1 1¼-ounce package taco
    seasoning mix
1 15.5-ounce can kidney beans
¼ teaspoon salt
1 large avocado, sliced
corn chips
tomato wedges

PLAY-BY-PLAY

1. Chop onion, lettuce and tomatoes. Toss with cheese, dressing and tabasco to taste.

2. Brown ground round, add taco seasoning mix. Add beans and salt, simmer for 10 minutes.

3. Combine beef and lettuce mixtures. Garnish with avocado, chips and tomato wedges and serve.

Serves 6

Andy and Lark MacPhail met at a Christmas party in 1979, but four years passed before they began dating, and another two before they were married. Now, together with their two young boys, William and Andrew, they make their year 'round home in the Twin Cities. Besides being with their children, Andy and Lark like to travel, go to restaurants, shop and discuss politics. "I do all the talking," confesses Lark. Andy loves to read in his spare time, and Lark likes swimming, playing tennis and watercolor painting. They dream of vacationing through Europe together. Andy's secret wish is to be a historian, and Lark's is to be an artist.

General Manager

Pepper Pasta Salad

from Rebecca and Robert Pohlad

LINE UP

3 tablespoons Dijon mustard
3 tablespoons freshly squeezed
    lemon juice
4 large cloves garlic, minced
    very fine
salt and freshly ground pepper
    to taste
½ cup olive oil

2 cups fresh broccoli florets
1 red pepper, chopped
8 ounces egg fettucine, cooked
    and drained well
8 ounces spinach fettucine,
    cooked and drained well
1 pound fresh mozzarella,
    coarsely chopped

PLAY-BY-PLAY

1. Combine mustard, lemon juice, garlic and salt and pepper. Add oil in steady stream, whisking constantly. Set aside.

2. Separately blanch broccoli and pepper in boiling water. Drain and rinse under cold water. Vegetables should remain crisp.

3. Toss pasta with vegetables and dressing. Sprinkle with cheese and serve immediately.

Serves 10

Tale of the Tape Tortellini

from Barbara and Mike Trombley

This pasta is great for parties or barbecues. Experiment with your favorite vegetables, cheese and olives. The salad keeps well in the refrigerator.

LINE UP

½ bunch broccoli, cut
    into florets
1 package Good Seasons Zesty
    Italian dressing mix
2 tablespoons water
½ cup oil
¼ cup vinegar

1 pound spiral pasta or fresh
    cheese-filled tortellini, or
    8 ounces of each, cooked
    and drained
1½ tomatoes, cubed
8 ounces medium cheddar or
    mozzarella cheese, cubed

PLAY-BY-PLAY

1. Steam broccoli florets, covered, in 1 inch of boiling water until bright green and still slightly crisp. Rinse in cold water and drain.

2. Prepare dressing according to package directions using water, oil and vinegar. Toss broccoli, pasta, tomatoes and cheese with dressing. Cover and chill for at least 1 hour before serving.

Serves 6

"It's a Tater" Potato Salad

from Bob Dorey

LINE UP

5 pounds potatoes
5 eggs
7 radishes, sliced
1 large onion, chopped
1 stalk celery, sliced

1 pint Miracle Whip salad
    dressing
2 tablespoons vinegar
3 tablespoons sugar
1 tablespoon mustard
salt and pepper

PLAY-BY-PLAY

1. In advance, prepare potatoes and eggs: Boil potatoes in skins and chill until cold. Hard-boil eggs and chill until cold.

2. Peel and dice potatoes. Peel and slice eggs. Combine potatoes, eggs, radishes, onion and celery.

3. Combine Miracle Whip, vinegar, sugar and mustard, mix until smooth. Pour over potatoes and mix well. Season to taste with salt and pepper.

Serves 24 (Feeds a team!)

Bob Dorey became the Twins clubhouse cook in 1985. Does he feel responsible for the two World Championships that came after he started cooking for the Twins? "Well, I don't get *too* many complaints," he says, "they're a good group of guys."

Hot German Potato Salad

from Jana and Jeff Reboulet

LINE UP

4 pounds potatoes
3 onions, chopped
¾ cup sugar
salt and pepper to taste
8 ounces diced bacon

¾ cup very hot water
¾ cup cider vinegar
4 hard-boiled eggs, halved
greens

PLAY-BY-PLAY

1. Boil potatoes until tender. While still warm, peel and slice into large mixing bowl.

2. Heap chopped onions in center of potatoes. Top with sugar, salt and pepper.

3. Fry bacon until crisp. Remove from pan and set aside. Add water and vinegar to bacon grease and bring to boil. Pour over potatoes and onions, tossing lightly to mix well.

4. Add bacon to potato salad. Serve garnished with egg halves and greens.

"yodelaieehoo!"

Serves 8

Grand Slammin' Salmon and Rice

from Nita and Harmon Killebrew

LINE UP

2 cups cooked and cooled
  white rice
1 cup sliced celery
½ cup sliced green onions
½ cup sweet pickle relish
1 cup salad dressing or
  mayonnaise

2 12½-ounce cans skinless,
  boneless pink salmon
½ cup chopped red pepper
½ cup pine nuts
1 cup frozen peas, thawed
½ teaspoon black pepper
18 lettuce leaves

PLAY-BY-PLAY

1. Combine all ingredients except for lettuce leaves and toss gently. Chill for at least 1½ hours.

2. To serve, place three lettuce leaves on plate. Mound salad on top of lettuce.

Serves 6

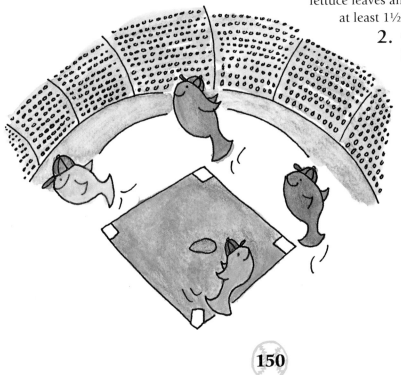

Keystone Taco Salad

from Chuck Knoblauch

LINE UP

2 pounds lean ground beef
1 large green pepper, diced
1 onion, diced
2 cloves garlic, minced
salt and pepper to taste
1 pound Velveeta cheese

1 10-ounce can diced tomatoes
   with chili
1 large head iceberg lettuce,
   coarsely chopped
2 large tomatoes, diced large
16 ounces Doritos, slightly
   crushed

PLAY-BY-PLAY

1. Cook beef, pepper, onion, and garlic in sauté pan until meat is brown. Season to taste with salt and pepper. Set aside.

2. Melt Velveeta cheese in top of double boiler or in microwave. Add canned tomatoes and mix until smooth.

3. In large serving bowl, combine lettuce and fresh tomatoes. Add Doritos and toss. Stir in meat. Top all with hot Velveeta and tomatoes, mix well.

Serves 10

Tips from Chuck's mom: "To mix the salad together is fine if everyone is ready to sit down to eat. But with so many eating at different times, and usually a ball game involved, I let the individuals mix their own. I use it as a main dish, with french bread and corn. As for the servings, it depends on who you are serving. Last spring this salad only fed me, my husband, Scott Leius and Chuck."

Lemonade Salad

from Lisa Limbaugh and Eddie Guardado

LINE UP

12 ounces Ritz crackers, crushed
1½ cups melted butter
1½ cups powdered sugar

1 14-ounce can sweetened
   condensed milk
12 ounces frozen lemonade
12 ounces Cool Whip, thawed

PLAY-BY-PLAY

1. Combine cracker crumbs and melted butter in 9-by-13-inch glass dish. Scatter to cover bottom of dish.

2. Combine sugar and milk, add lemonade and mix until lemonade is melted. Fold in Cool Whip and pour over cracker-butter mixture. Freeze overnight.

3. Before serving, let dessert stand at room temperature or in refrigerator for 30 minutes. Store in freezer.

Serves 12

"Who us? A salad?"

"Don't be so sour!"

*Michelle, Larry,
and Kayley*

Bullpen Baked Beans

from Michelle and Larry Casian

LINE UP

36 ounces canned pork and beans   ½ cup ketchup
¾ cup brown sugar   6 slices bacon, cut into pieces
1 teaspoon mustard

PLAY-BY-PLAY

1. Preheat oven to 325 degrees. Grease 2-quart casserole.
Combine brown sugar and mustard.

2. Pour half of beans into casserole. Sprinkle with half of brown
sugar mixture. Repeat. Pour ketchup over all, then sprinkle with
bacon.

3. Bake for 2½ hours, stirring occasionally.

Serves 8

Soak dried beans overnight to shorten cooking time: Rinse and pick over beans. Place in large bowl and cover with 3 inches cool water. The next day, drain beans and rinse again. Use fresh water to cook as directed in your recipe—beans will be tender in about 45 minutes.

To release the most flavorful garlic oils, always crush the cloves: Slice cloves in half and place cut side down on cutting board. Rest broad knife blade over garlic and press down with heel of hand. Be careful, garlic may be slippery. Chop or mince garlic as directed in your recipe.

Tony O's Black Beans

from Gordette and Tony Oliva

LINE UP

1 pound black beans
1 tablespoon salt
1 bay leaf
1 tablespoon oregano
¼ teaspoon cumin
½ teaspoon sugar
1 teaspoon bacon grease

1 tablespoon olive oil
1 onion, chopped
2 cloves garlic, crushed and
    chopped
½ green pepper, chopped
4 cups cooked white rice

PLAY-BY-PLAY

1. Boil beans in salted water until tender, about 2 hours. Add bay leaf, oregano, cumin and sugar.

2. Heat bacon grease and olive oil in sauté pan. Add onion, garlic and green pepper, cook about 5 minutes.

3. Add sautéed vegetables to beans and simmer 30 minutes longer. Adjust seasoning to taste and serve over white rice.

Serves 6

Hot Corner Potatoes

from Karen and Mike Pagliarulo

This side dish can be prepared ahead and frozen or refrigerated. Remember that a cold or frozen dish will take more time to bake.

LINE UP

2½ pounds potatoes, cubed large
3 tablespoons butter
3 tablespoons flour
¼ cup sherry or white wine
3 cups milk, warmed

*10 ounces American or cheddar
  cheese, cubed*
*½ cup white and wheat
  bread crumbs*

PLAY-BY-PLAY

1. Boil potatoes until just tender, about 15 minutes. Drain and place in 2-quart casserole. Preheat oven to 350 degrees.

2. Melt butter in large saucepan over low heat. Add flour, whisking constantly, cooking until golden. Gradually add sherry or wine. Whisk until smooth, then begin gradually adding milk. Whisk until all milk is smoothly incorporated.

3. Bring sauce just to a boil, then add cheese. Stir and cook until cheese melts. Pour sauce over potatoes in casserole. Sprinkle with bread crumbs and bake for 30 minutes.

Serves 6

T. Rex's Creamed Corn

from Jeanie and Kent Hrbek

Goes great with barbecued chicken or steaks.

LINE UP

40 ounces frozen kernel corn	2 tablespoons sugar
1 cup whipping cream	pinch white or cayenne pepper
1 cup milk	2 tablespoons melted butter
1 teaspoon salt	2 tablespoons flour

PLAY-BY-PLAY

1. Combine corn, cream, milk, salt, sugar and pepper in sauce pan. Bring to boil, reduce heat and simmer 5 minutes.

2. Add melted butter and flour to corn. Mix well. Remove from heat and serve.

Serves 6-8

Kent and Jeanie Hrbek met through her father, with special thanks to a big buck who provided the opportunity as well as plenty of venison. Jeanie's father was camped next to Kent's party on a hunting trip. Kent got to talking with her father and discovered they were neighbors. Kent was invited over to help clean the deer, and Kent and Jeanie were introduced. Before the next deer season, they were dating. Both the Hrbeks share a love of the outdoors, with camping, fishing and hunting among their favorite things to do together. They make their home in Minnesota along with daughter Heidi.

14   First Base

Rounding Third Cheese Potatoes

from Carol and Ron Gardenhire

> ❝ I make these potatoes every time an invitation includes bringing a covered dish. It's always a hit! ❞
>
> —Carol Gardenhire

LINE UP

2 pounds frozen hashbrowns, thawed
1 teaspoon salt
¼ teaspoon pepper
½ cup margarine
1 can cream of mushroom soup

2 cups grated marble cheese
6 ounces sour cream with chives
¼ chopped onion
2 cups crushed corn flakes
¼ cup melted margarine

PLAY-BY-PLAY

1. Preheat oven to 350 degrees.

2. Combine potatoes with salt and pepper. Melt margarine in saucepan, add soup, cheese, sour cream and onion. Stir and warm until mixed well.

3. Combine potatoes with warm sauce in 9-by-13-inch baking pan.

4. Mix corn flakes with melted margarine and sprinkle over top of potatoes. Bake for 45 minutes.

Serves 6-8

Mashed Potatoes with a Twist

from Monica and David McCarty

LINE UP

5 Idaho potatoes, peeled and cubed
½ cup milk
2 tablespoons butter or margarine
2 tablespoons olive oil
5 large mushrooms, chopped

¼ cup chopped onion
4 cloves garlic, crushed
¼ cup freshly grated parmesan cheese
1 teaspoon parsley
salt and pepper to taste

PLAY-BY-PLAY

1. Boil potatoes until very tender. Drain and mash with milk and butter. Cover and set aside.

2. Heat olive oil in sauté pan and cook mushrooms, onion and garlic until soft, 5 minutes.

3. Fold vegetables and all seasonings into potatoes. Serve immediately.

Serves 4

Scalloped Potatoes and Ham

from Michelle and Larry Casian

LINE UP

¼ cup butter
2 tablespoons plus 1½ teaspoons
    flour
2 cups milk
salt and pepper to taste

¼ cup cubed American cheese
¼ cup cubed cheddar cheese
9 potatoes, cubed and cooked
1 pound ham steak, cubed

PLAY-BY-PLAY

1. Preheat oven to 350 degrees.

2. Melt butter in saucepan. Gradually add flour, stirring and heating until smooth. Carefully add milk, stirring constantly until sauce is consistency of gravy. Season with salt and pepper.

3. Add cheeses to sauce. Stir until melted. Place potatoes and ham into glass baking dish, pour sauce over. Bake for 30 minutes.

Serves 6

❝ I'm not much of a cook and we are all picky eaters. So I like simple recipes. Most of the dishes I cook were given to me by Larry's mom or mine. Larry's father is Mexican, so he grew up eating a lot of Mexican food. ❞

—Michelle Casian

Larry and Michelle Casian were both born and raised in sunny Southern California, where they met in a high school biology class. Today, they live in Salem, Oregon with daughter Kayley, a busy youngster who loves Minnesota's zoos and Camp Snoopy. Michelle says, "I wish I had more time to cook, but baseball makes for a crazy schedule." In the future, Larry hopes to open a pitching school. Both the Casians want to teach some day. They love to travel and dream of vacationing in Australia, Hawaii and the Caribbean.

48 Pitcher

Free-wheeling adventure is the name of the game for Brett and Rosemary Merriman. They love camping, four-wheeling and riding ATVs. Their dream vacation? The wilds of Australia. Sports, food and fun all score big with Brett. If he weren't involved in baseball, he'd like "to own a sports bar and grill." Chandler, Arizona is home for the Merrimans and their son Alec Trey.

47 Pitcher

Twice Baked Potatoes

from Rosemary and Brett Merriman

LINE UP

4 large baking potatoes
3 tablespoons butter, melted
½ cup milk

¼ cup sour cream
salt and pepper to taste
1 cup shredded cheddar cheese

PLAY-BY-PLAY

1. Preheat oven to 350 degrees. Bake potatoes for 1 hour. Cool.

2. Slice potatoes in half lengthwise. Hollow out middle of potato and remove to a mixing bowl. Add butter, milk and sour cream. Season with salt and pepper.

3. Fill potato skins with mixture and sprinkle with cheese. Arrange potatoes on a baking sheet and bake for 10 minutes.

Serves 4

Baked Spinach with Bacon

from Lark and Andy MacPhail

LINE UP

3 cups cooked, drained spinach
2 cups drained canned tomatoes
1 onion, chopped
¼ cup chili sauce
1 cup cracker crumbs, reserving
    2 tablespoons

1 teaspoon salt
¼ teaspoon paprika
8 ounces shredded American
    cheese
6 slices bacon

“ I made this to bring to my Mom's house for Thanksgiving. Everyone loved it! ”

—Danielle Parks

PLAY-BY-PLAY

1. Preheat oven to 350 degrees. Grease 2-quart baking dish.

2. Using a small portion of each ingredient, layer spinach, tomatoes, onion, chili sauce and cracker crumbs in baking dish. Sprinkle lightly with salt, pepper and cheese. Repeat layers as needed. Top with reserved 2 tablespoons cracker crumbs.

3. Arrange bacon slices over the casserole and bake for 25 minutes.

Serves 6

WHO'S WHO

19

20

21

See page 239

Sweet Spot
Desserts

Sweet Spot Desserts

Sweet Spot Desserts

Clubhouse Applesauce Cake

from Bob Dorey

To measure flour accurately, use graduated dry measuring cups. Mound flour lightly into the size cup called for. Do not pack, tap or shake. Level off excess with a straight metal spatula. Use this same method for measuring spices and leavening agents.

LINE UP

1½ cups applesauce
1 teaspoon baking soda
1 cup sugar
½ cup shortening
1 egg
2 cups flour

½ teaspoon salt
1 teaspoon each: cinnamon,
    cloves and nutmeg
1 cup raisins
1 cup walnuts or pecans

PLAY-BY-PLAY

1. Preheat oven to 350 degrees. Grease 9-by-13-inch baking pan. Dissolve baking soda in applesauce, set aside.

2. Cream sugar and shortening. Add egg and applesauce with baking soda. Mix well.

3. Sift flour with salt and spices. Blend into batter. Stir in raisins and nuts. Pour into pan and bake for 50-60 minutes. If desired, frost cooled cake with a cream cheese frosting.

Serves 12

Hershey's Disappearing Cake

from Robin and Lenny Webster

LINE UP

¾ cup butter, softened
¼ cup shortening
2 cups sugar
2 teaspoons vanilla
2 eggs
1 cup Hershey's cocoa

1¾ cups flour
¾ teaspoon baking powder
¾ teaspoon baking soda
dash salt
1¾ cups plus 2 tablespoons milk
2 cups powdered sugar

This is Lenny and Robin's favorite cake. Although she bakes it for the holidays, Robin says, "I never get more than one slice."

PLAY-BY-PLAY

1. Preheat oven to 350 degrees. Grease and flour two 9-inch round cake pans.

2. Cream ¼ cup of the butter, shortening, sugar and 1 teaspoon of the vanilla until fluffy. Blend in eggs.

3. Combine ¾ cup of the cocoa, flour, baking powder, baking soda and salt. Add to butter mixture alternately with 1¾ cups of the milk. Blend well and divide between cake pans.

4. Bake cakes for 30-35 minutes, until toothpick inserted in center comes out clean. Cool 10 minutes. Remove cakes from pans.

5. Beat together remaining ½ cup butter, ¼ cup cocoa, 1 teaspoon vanilla and powdered sugar. Add remaining 2 tablespoons milk to desired consistency for frosting. Blend well until very smooth. Fill and frost cooled cake.

Serves 8

Chocolate Caramel Cake

from Cori and Pat Meares

LINE UP

1 18.25-ounce package chocolate
  cake mix
14 ounces caramels, unwrapped

1 14-ounce can sweetened
  condensed milk
½ cup margarine
1 cup coarsely chopped pecans

PLAY-BY-PLAY

1. Preheat oven to 350 degrees. Grease 9-by-13-inch baking pan.

2. Prepare cake as directed on package. Spread 2 cups of batter into pan and bake for 15 minutes.

3. Meanwhile, in heavy saucepan over low heat, melt caramels with condensed milk and margarine. Spread evenly over baked cake layer. Cover caramel with remaining cake batter and sprinkle nuts over all.

4. Bake until cake springs back when lightly touched, 30-35 minutes. Cool before serving.

Serves 8

Home Run Honey Cream Cheesecake

from Sherry and Rick Aguilera

LINE UP

1¼ cups graham cracker crumbs
⅓ cup melted butter
2 tablespoons sugar
1 pound cream cheese, softened

⅔ cup honey, plus more to taste
2 eggs
2 teaspoons vanilla
2 cups sour cream

❝ Rick's favorite dessert! ❞

—Sherry Aguilera

PLAY-BY-PLAY

1. Preheat oven to 325 degrees.

2. Combine graham cracker crumbs, melted butter and sugar. Press into the bottom and up the sides of 9 or 10-inch springform pan.

3. Blend cream cheese, ⅓ cup of the honey, eggs and vanilla. Pour into crust. Bake until center seems set, about 30 minutes. Remove from oven.

4. Blend sour cream with remaining ⅓ cup honey until smooth. Spread over cake. Return to oven to set cream, about 15 minutes.

5. Let cool and chill up to 1 day. Drizzle with additional honey before serving.

Serves 12

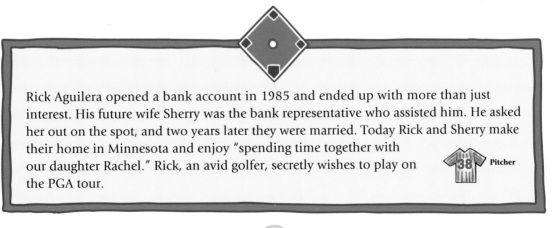

Rick Aguilera opened a bank account in 1985 and ended up with more than just interest. His future wife Sherry was the bank representative who assisted him. He asked her out on the spot, and two years later they were married. Today Rick and Sherry make their home in Minnesota and enjoy "spending time together with our daughter Rachel." Rick, an avid golfer, secretly wishes to play on the PGA tour.

38 Pitcher

As a newlywed, Gene took two bites of wife Kathleen's first attempt at a gourmet meal and walked out the door. Ten minutes later he returned to his shocked wife with a large pizza in hand. "He said he couldn't find the words to describe how awful the dinner was, so he decided to provide us with something edible." Things have improved dramatically since then—try these luxurious cheesecakes and see for yourself!

Mini-Cheesecakes

from Kathleen and Gene Larkin

LINE UP

24 aluminum cupcake cups
24 vanilla wafers
1 pound cream cheese, softened
¾ cup sugar

2 eggs
1 teaspoon vanilla
1 21-ounce can fruit filling

PLAY-BY-PLAY

1. Preheat oven to 350 degrees. Arrange aluminum cups on baking sheet. Put one vanilla wafer at the bottom of each cup.

2. Beat cream cheese, sugar, eggs and vanilla. Pour into cups, filling each a generous two-thirds full. Bake for 15 minutes.

3. Remove cheesecakes from oven. Cool. Top with fruit filling.

Makes 2 dozen mini-cheesecakes

Coach's Coconut Cake

from Carol and Ron Gardenhire

This recipe is from Drenda, my neighbor in Roseville. She's made us many cakes and breads; this one is our favorite. It's very rich and very good. Thank you Drenda— you're wonderful!

LINE UP

1 18.5-ounce package yellow
    cake mix
1 15-ounce can cream of coconut

1 14-ounce can sweetened
    condensed milk
8 ounces Cool Whip, thawed
7 ounces flaked coconut

PLAY-BY-PLAY

1. Bake cake as directed on package for 9-by-13-inch baking pan. Pierce baked cake all over with fork to create small holes.

2. Slowly pour cream of coconut over warm cake, allowing cream to seep into cake. Pour condensed milk over coconut-soaked cake; let cool.

3. Spread Cool Whip over cake and sprinkle with coconut.

Serves 12

Chocolate Truffle Cake

from Barbara and Mike Trombley

> " My Dad,
> Robert Pecht, is
> a pastry chef for
> a large hotel-
> conference
> center. He made
> Chocolate Truffle
> Cake in 1991
> for a reception
> honoring
> President Bush. "
>
> —Barbara Trombley

You can use two 18.25-ounce packages of chocolate cake mix for the four layers in this strictly chocolate cake. Serve it with vanilla ice cream.

LINE UP

2¼ cups heavy cream
1½ pounds semisweet chocolate,
   broken into pieces
5 tablespoons rum extract

2 recipes chocolate layer cake,
   prepared into 4 layers and
   cooled

PLAY-BY-PLAY

1. Begin one day before serving. Grease 9-inch springform pan.

2. Bring 1½ cups of the cream to rapid boil. Pour over 1 pound of the semisweet chocolate. Add 3 tablespoons rum extract and stir until chocolate melts. Cool.

3. Break up cakes and place in large mixing bowl. Add cooled chocolate-cream mixture. Beat on medium until smooth. Mixture will be thick.

4. Spread chocolate mixture into springform pan and refrigerate overnight.

5. The next day, bring remaining ¾ cup cream to rapid boil. Pour over remaining ½ pound semisweet chocolate. Add remaining 2 tablespoons rum extract and stir until chocolate melts.

6. Run knife between cake and pan, loosen clasp and remove cake to wire rack. Pour chocolate-cream mixture over cake and refrigerate until serving.

Serves 16

Big Hit Sour Cream Coffee Cake

from Nita and Harmon Killebrew

LINE UP

2 cups flour
1 teaspoon baking powder
1 teaspoon baking soda
½ cup butter, softened
1 cup plus 2 tablespoons sugar
2 eggs
4 ounces sour cream
1 teaspoon vanilla
¼ teaspoon lemon juice
1½ teaspoons cinnamon
½ cup finely chopped walnuts or pecans

PLAY-BY-PLAY

1. Preheat oven to 350 degrees. Grease and flour 9-inch tube pan.

2. Combine flour, baking powder and baking soda, set aside. Cream butter and 1 cup of the sugar. Add eggs.

3. Add dry ingredients to butter mixture alternately with sour cream. Beat until smooth. Stir in vanilla and lemon juice.

4. In small bowl, combine remaining 2 tablespoons sugar, cinnamon and chopped nuts.

5. Spread half of the cake batter in pan. Sprinkle with half the nut mixture. Cover with remaining batter and sprinkle remaining nut mixture over all. Bake for 45 minutes.

Serves 10

Cinnamon Crumb Coffee Cake

from Barbara and Mike Trombley

> **This is a favorite recipe from my Mom's side of the family. I love to bake it for breakfast or around the holidays.**
>
> —Barbara Trombley

LINE UP

1 cup margarine, softened
2 eggs
1½ cups sugar
1 teaspoon vanilla

3 cups flour
2 teaspoons baking powder
½ teaspoon salt
1 cup milk
2 teaspoons cinnamon

PLAY-BY-PLAY

1. Preheat oven to 350 degrees. Grease and flour 9-by-13-inch glass baking pan.

2. In large mixing bowl, combine ½ cup of the margarine, eggs, ½ cup of the sugar and vanilla until smooth. Add 2 cups of the flour, baking powder and salt alternately with milk to make a smooth batter. Spread in baking pan.

3. Combine remaining ½ cup margarine, 1 cup sugar, 1 cup flour and cinnamon, using fingers until mixture has a crumb-like consistency. Crumb mixture should be dry, but stick together if squeezed in hand. If too wet, add a little more flour. Sprinkle over batter. Bake for 25-30 minutes.

Serves 9

The weight room at Duke University was the romantic setting where Mike and Barbara Trombley met. He was training for baseball and she was training for track. Today they like to play golf, travel and "root for Duke." Fishing and collecting baseball memorabilia are Mike's favorite hobbies. Barbara likes to bake, thanks to her sweet heritage — both her father and grandfather were pastry chefs. The Trombleys enjoy a traditional Polish feast on Christmas Eve. Mike's grandmother makes all his favorites — borscht, perogies and kielbasa. Mike dreams of one day playing on the PGA tour. For now, he'll settle for a golf vacation in Hawaii.

21 **Pitcher**

Piña Colada Cake

from Jana and Jeff Reboulet

Use either a 9-by-13-inch or two 9-inch cake pans for this rummy dessert.

LINE UP

1 18.25-ounce package white cake mix

2 3.4-ounce packages instant coconut cream pudding mix

4 eggs

½ cup plus ⅓ cup rum

¼ cup oil

1 8-ounce can crushed pineapple in juice, drained

8 ounces Cool Whip, thawed

PLAY-BY-PLAY

1. Preheat oven to 350 degrees. Grease and flour one 9-by-13-inch or two 9-inch cake pans.

2. Combine cake mix, 1 package instant pudding mix, eggs, ½ cup of the rum and oil. Mix well. Pour into pan(s) and bake for 25-30 minutes. Cool.

3. Combine remaining package instant pudding mix, remaining ⅓ cup rum, and pineapple. Fold in Cool Whip and frost cooled cake. Keep cake refrigerated.

Serves 10-12

Streusel-Filled Coffee Cake

from Donna and Greg Brummett

LINE UP

1½ cups plus 2 tablespoons flour
½ cup brown sugar
2 teaspoons cinnamon
2 tablespoons melted butter
1 tablespoon baking powder
½ teaspoon salt

¾ cup sugar
¼ cup shortening
1 egg
½ cup milk
1 teaspoon vanilla

PLAY-BY-PLAY

1. Preheat oven to 375 degrees. Grease 8-inch square baking pan. For streusel mix, combine 2 tablespoons of the flour, brown sugar, cinnamon and melted butter. Set aside.

2. Sift together remaining 1½ cups flour, baking powder, salt and sugar. Cut in shortening. Mix in egg and milk. Blend well, add vanilla.

3. Pour half of batter into baking pan. Sprinkle with half of the streusel mix. Repeat layers. Bake for 25-30 minutes.

Serves 6

Grandma May's Apple Cake

from Nita and Harmon Killebrew

LINE UP

2¼ cups sugar
1 teaspoon cinnamon
3 cups flour
pinch salt
1 tablespoon baking soda

1 cup oil
2½ teaspoons vanilla
4 eggs
½ cup orange juice
4 apples, peeled, cored and
    sliced thin

PLAY-BY-PLAY

1. Preheat oven to 350 degrees. Grease well 12-cup tube pan. Combine ¼ cup of the sugar with cinnamon and set aside.

2. Combine remaining 2 cups sugar with rest of ingredients except apples. Mix well. Spread half of the cake batter in tube pan. Arrange half of the sliced apples over batter. Sprinkle with half of the sugar-cinnamon mixture.

3. Repeat layers with remaining batter, apples, and sugar-cinnamon. Bake 1½ hours or until toothpick inserted near center comes out clean.

4. Remove from oven and let stand for 20 minutes. Loosen cake from sides of pan with knife, then invert onto serving platter.

Serves 8-10

Harvey Wall Banger Cake

from Jana and Jeff Reboulet

The Reboulets do a lot of wall banging in their spare time, as remodeling is one of their favorite pastimes. "Our new home needed a lot of updating and that took up most of last year's and this year's off-seasons," explains Jana. "When I'm not working on the house or taking care of the family, I like to read and ride my bike."

LINE UP

1 18.25-ounce box orange cake mix
1 3.4-ounce box instant vanilla pudding
½ cup vegetable oil
4 eggs

¾ cup plus 1½ tablespoons orange juice
¼ cup plus 1½ tablespoons vodka
¼ cup plus 1½ tablespoons Galliano
1 cup powdered sugar

PLAY-BY-PLAY

1. Preheat oven to 350 degrees. Grease and flour tube pan.

2. Beat cake mix, instant pudding, oil, eggs, ¾ cup of the orange juice, ¼ cup of the vodka and ¼ cup of the Galliano for 4 minutes. Spread in pan and bake for 45-55 minutes.

3. Meanwhile, combine remaining 1½ tablespoons orange juice, 1½ tablespoons vodka and 1½ tablespoons Galliano with powdered sugar. Stir until smooth.

4. Let cake cool for 10 minutes. Invert onto wire rack and drizzle warm cake with icing.

Serves 8

½ tablespoon = 1½ teaspoons.

Pohlad's Pepsi Cake

from Rebecca and Robert Pohlad

LINE UP

½ cup buttermilk
1 teaspoon baking soda
2 cups flour
2 cups sugar
1½ cups butter
¼ cup plus 2 tablespoons cocoa

1¼ cup plus 2 tablespoons Pepsi
2 eggs
2 teaspoons vanilla
1½ cups miniature
    marshmallows
1 pound powdered sugar

PLAY-BY-PLAY

1. Preheat oven to 350 degrees. Grease 9-by-13-inch baking pan.

2. Dissolve baking soda in buttermilk and set aside. Sift together flour and sugar and set aside.

3. Combine 1 cup of the butter, 3 tablespoons of the cocoa and 1 cup of the Pepsi in saucepan and bring to rapid boil. Remove to a mixing bowl and add flour and sugar.

4. Stir in buttermilk-baking soda mixture, eggs and 1 teaspoon of the vanilla. Mix well and add marshmallows. Spread in pan and bake for 35-40 minutes.

5. Meanwhile, combine remaining ½ cup butter, 3 tablespoons cocoa and 6 tablespoons Pepsi in saucepan and bring to a boil. Remove to mixing bowl and add 1 teaspoon vanilla and powdered sugar. Mix well and spread over hot cake.

Serves 12

Killer Pumpkin Pound Cake with Walnut Sauce

from Nita and Harmon Killebrew

Baking this cake fills your kitchen with the warm, cozy smell of sweet spices and pumpkin that will entice your family and friends. Use a pastry brush to remove any extra flour from the outside of the cake.

LINE UP

*1½ cups plus 2 tablespoons butter or margarine,
    softened*
2¾ cups sugar
1½ teaspoons vanilla
6 eggs
3 cups flour
½ teaspoon baking powder
½ teaspoon plus a dash salt
¾ teaspoon cinnamon
¼ teaspoon cloves
1 cup canned pumpkin
1 cup brown sugar
¼ cup dark corn syrup
½ cup heavy cream
½ cup chopped walnuts or walnut halves

PLAY-BY-PLAY

1. Preheat oven to 350 degrees. Generously grease and lightly flour 12-cup fluted tube pan.

2. Cream 1½ cups of the butter with sugar until light and fluffy. Add 1 teaspoon of the vanilla and the eggs, one at a time, beating well after each addition.

3. Combine flour, baking powder, ½ teaspoon of the salt and the spices. Add dry ingredients alternately with pumpkin to the batter, blending well after each addition.

4. Pour batter into pan and bake until toothpick inserted near center comes out clean, 60-70 minutes. Cool for 15 minutes; invert onto serving platter.

5. Meanwhile, combine remaining 2 tablespoons butter, remaining dash salt, brown sugar, corn syrup and cream in small saucepan over medium heat. Cook, stirring constantly, until boiling. Reduce heat to low and simmer for 5 minutes, stirring constantly.

6. Remove from heat and stir in remaining ½ teaspoon vanilla and walnuts. Let cool until sauce is warm and thick. Slice warm cake and spoon walnut sauce over each piece.

Serves 10

❝ Baseball, my son, is the cornerstone of civilization. ❞

—Dagwood Bumstead, as drawn by Chic Young

Plum Nutty Cake

from Nancy and John Gordon

LINE UP

2 cups sifted self-rising flour
2 cups sugar
½ teaspoon cinnamon
½ teaspoon cloves
¼ teaspoon nutmeg
¾ cup oil

3 eggs
2 4-ounce jars plum baby food
1 cup chopped pecans
½ cup powdered sugar
3-4 tablespoons lemon juice

PLAY-BY-PLAY

1. Preheat oven to 325 degrees. Grease tube pan well.

2. Combine all ingredients except powdered sugar and lemon juice. Mix well and pour into pan. Bake for 1 hour and 10 minutes. Cool for 10 minutes; invert cake onto serving platter.

3. Combine powdered sugar with enough lemon juice to form a thin glaze. Drizzle cake with lemon glaze.

Serves 10

Rick, Kathie, and Michael

Good Pitch Pineapple Cake

from Kathie and Rick Stelmaszek

> ❝ This recipe was handed down from my grandmother. ❞
>
> —Kathie Stelmaszek

LINE UP

2 tablespoons cornstarch
1¼ cup sugar
2 cups canned crushed pineapple
1 egg white
¼ teaspoon cream of tartar
1 teaspoon vanilla
¼ cup boiling water
2 9-inch round layers white cake
½ cup coconut

PLAY-BY-PLAY

1. Combine cornstarch and ½ cup of the sugar in saucepan. Add pineapple with canning juice and cook slowly over low heat until clear and thick. Cool and spread between cake layers.

2. Combine egg white, remaining ¾ cup sugar, cream of tartar and vanilla in mixing bowl. Add boiling water and beat on high speed to stiff peaks.

3. Frost cake, sprinkle with coconut and serve.

Serves 10

Strawberry Nut Cake

from Robin and Lenny Webster

To prepare cake pans, always grease and flour the bottoms. Cakes grip the sides of pan while baking and pull away from sides of pan when done. If at all, the cake will stick to the bottom of the pan.

LINE UP

1 18.25-ounce white cake mix
1 3-ounce box strawberry jello
1 cup vegetable oil
1½ cups frozen strawberries
½ cup milk
4 eggs

1½ cups flaked coconut
1½ cups pecans, chopped
1 pound powdered sugar
½ cup butter or margarine, melted

PLAY-BY-PLAY

1. Preheat oven to 350 degrees. Grease and flour bottoms of three 8-inch cake pans.

2. Combine white cake mix, jello, oil, 1 cup of the frozen strawberries, milk, eggs, 1 cup of the flaked coconut and 1 cup of the pecans. Mix well and divide between pans.

3. Bake cakes for 25-30 minutes. Remove from oven and cool 5 minutes on wire rack. Remove cakes from pans and let cool completely.

4. Meanwhile, combine powdered sugar, butter, remaining ½ cup strawberries, remaining ½ cup pecans and remaining ½ cup coconut. Mix well and use to fill layers and ice top and sides of cooled cake.

Serves 8-10

Apricot Squares

from Kathie and Rick Stelmaszek

LINE UP

1 cup margarine, softened
1 cup brown sugar
2 cups flour
1 cup chopped walnuts

24 ounces canned apricot filling
8 ounces cream cheese, softened
1 cup powdered sugar
16 ounces Cool Whip, thawed

PLAY-BY-PLAY

1. Preheat oven to 350 degrees. Lightly grease a cookie sheet.

2. Cream margarine and brown sugar. Add flour and walnuts, mix well. Break mixture into pieces and pat down onto prepared cookie sheet to form crust. Bake for 18 minutes. Cool.

3. Spread apricot filling over cooled crust. Bake 5 minutes more. Cool.

4. Combine cream cheese and powdered sugar. Carefully spread over apricot filling.

5. Smooth Cool Whip over all. Chill. When cold, cut into small squares and serve.

Makes 30 squares

"Spending seven days doing absolutely nothing," is Rick Stelmaszek's idea of the perfect vacation. Rick met his wife Kathie when they were both in grammar school. Now their own son Michael is in grammar school. Rick enjoys racquetball and relaxes by watching old movies. The Stelmaszeks are, however, adventurous when it comes to food. They love to find "good, out-of-the-way neighborhood restaurants." Rick's secret desire is "to become a frugal gourmet" and someday build his own house.

43 **Bullpen Coach**

Twin Chocolate Brownies

from Sharon and Kevin Tapani

❝ **Really an easy no-fuss treat.** ❞

—Sharon Tapani

LINE UP

1 cup margarine	1 teaspoon baking powder
½ cup cocoa	1 teaspoon salt
2 cups sugar	1 1.55-ounce bar Hershey's
1 teaspoon vanilla	dark chocolate
4 eggs	3 tablespoons milk
1½ cups flour	1½ cups powdered sugar

PLAY-BY-PLAY

1. Preheat oven to 350 degrees. Grease 9-by-13-inch baking pan.

2. Melt ¾ cup of the margarine in small sauce pan. Add cocoa and sugar and mix over low heat until well blended and dissolved. Remove to mixing bowl.

3. Add vanilla, then eggs one at a time to cocoa mixture. Mix well. Blend in flour, baking powder and salt. Turn into baking dish and bake for 30 minutes.

4. After the brownies are done, melt remaining ¼ cup margarine with chocolate over low heat. Beat in milk and powdered sugar. Spread on warm brownies.

Makes 16-20 brownies

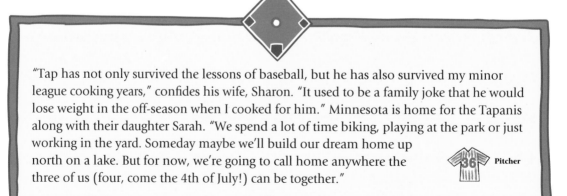

"Tap has not only survived the lessons of baseball, but he has also survived my minor league cooking years," confides his wife, Sharon. "It used to be a family joke that he would lose weight in the off-season when I cooked for him." Minnesota is home for the Tapanis along with their daughter Sarah. "We spend a lot of time biking, playing at the park or just working in the yard. Someday maybe we'll build our dream home up north on a lake. But for now, we're going to call home anywhere the three of us (four, come the 4th of July!) can be together."

36 Pitcher

Butter Cookies

from Judi and Chip Hale

LINE UP

1 cup butter, softened
1 cup sugar
2 beaten egg yolks
1 teaspoon vanilla
2½ cups flour

PLAY-BY-PLAY

1. Preheat oven to 375 degrees.

2. Cream butter and sugar. Add egg yolks and vanilla and mix well. Gradually add flour.

3. Form dough into balls the size of walnuts and place 2 inches apart on cookie sheets. Flatten with fork.

4. Bake for 8-10 minutes, until golden. Remove from oven, let rest 2 minutes before removing cookies to wire racks to cool completely.

Makes 40 cookies

Judi, Chip, and Jack

❝ We baked these on our first date. ❞

—Judi Hale

"Touch 'em All!" Chocolate Bars

from Nancy and John Gordon

LINE UP

1 cup plus 2 tablespoons
    margarine
2 cups brown sugar
2 eggs
2 teaspoons vanilla
1 teaspoon salt

1 teaspoon baking soda
2¼ cups flour
2 cups oatmeal
1 14-ounce can sweetened
    condensed milk
12 ounces chocolate chips

PLAY-BY-PLAY

1. Preheat oven to 350 degrees. Grease 9-by-13-inch baking pan.

2. Cream 1 cup of the margarine with brown sugar. Blend in eggs, 1 teaspoon of the vanilla and salt. Stir in baking soda, flour and oatmeal. Spread two-thirds of dough into pan.

3. In heavy saucepan combine remaining 2 tablespoons margarine, condensed milk and chocolate. Heat over low until melted, stirring constantly. Stir in remaining 1 teaspoon vanilla.

4. Spread chocolate mixture over dough. Drop remaining dough by teaspoons on top of chocolate layer. Bake for 25 minutes. Cool before cutting.

Makes about 40 bars

Great Scott's Chocolate Chip Cookies

from Scott Erickson

LINE UP

2 cups butter, softened
1½ cups sugar
1½ cups brown sugar
4 eggs
1 tablespoon vanilla

4½ cups flour
1 cup instant oatmeal, ground
2 teaspoons baking soda
36 ounces chocolate chips

PLAY-BY-PLAY

1. Preheat oven to 375 degrees.

2. Cream butter with sugars until light. Add eggs and vanilla, mix well. Stir in flour, oatmeal and baking soda until mixed through. Stir in chocolate chips.

3. Drop by large spoonfuls onto cookie sheets. Bake for 8-10 minutes.

Makes 5 dozen cookies

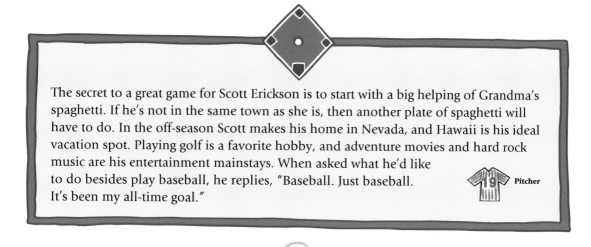

The secret to a great game for Scott Erickson is to start with a big helping of Grandma's spaghetti. If he's not in the same town as she is, then another plate of spaghetti will have to do. In the off-season Scott makes his home in Nevada, and Hawaii is his ideal vacation spot. Playing golf is a favorite hobby, and adventure movies and hard rock music are his entertainment mainstays. When asked what he'd like to do besides play baseball, he replies, "Baseball. Just baseball. It's been my all-time goal."

19 Pitcher

"This is a farmer's wife's recipe. It's about 40 years old," says Marge. Toast the walnuts in the oven before adding to the cookies—the flavor is wonderful.

Home Game Chocolate Chip Cookies

from Marge and Jim Wiesner

LINE UP

1 teaspoon baking soda
1 teaspoon warm water
1 cup shortening
¾ cup brown sugar
¾ cup sugar
2 eggs

1 teaspoon vanilla
2½ cups flour
1 cup chopped walnuts or
    pecans, if desired
½ teaspoon salt
9 ounces chocolate chips

PLAY-BY-PLAY

1. Preheat oven to 375 degrees. Dissolve baking soda in water.

2. Cream shortening and sugars until light. Add eggs, soda and water, and vanilla. Stir in flour, nuts, salt and chocolate chips.

3. Drop by rounded teaspoonfuls onto cookie sheets. Bake for 10 minutes, until lightly brown.

Makes 3½ dozen cookies

Chip's Chocolate Raspberry Bars

from Judi and Chip Hale

LINE UP

12 ounces chocolate chips
¼ cup butter
1 cup sugar
4 eggs, separated and whites
    stiffly beaten

2 tablespoons flour
1 cup raspberry jam, warmed
1½ cups heavy cream
1 teaspoon vanilla
1 teaspoon instant coffee

PLAY-BY-PLAY

1. Preheat oven to 350 degrees. Grease and flour bottom of 9-by-13-inch baking pan.

2. In small saucepan, melt 5 ounces of the chocolate chips with butter over low heat. Remove to mixing bowl and let cool 5 minutes.

3. Add sugar and egg yolks to chocolate-butter mixture, beat well. Stir in flour. Gently fold in egg whites.

4. Spread into baking pan and bake for 20-25 minutes, until cake pulls away from the edge of the pan and springs to the touch. Remove from oven and spread warm raspberry jam over top. Let cool.

5. Whip 1 cup of the heavy cream and spread over raspberry layer. Refrigerate for 1 hour.

6. Meanwhile, melt remaining 7 ounces chocolate chips in double boiler with remaining ½ cup heavy cream, vanilla and instant coffee. Let cool, then drizzle over cool dessert.

Serves 12

Going...Going...Gone! Ginger Snaps

from Rebecca and Robert Pohlad

LINE UP

¾ cup shortening
1 cup sugar
¼ cup molasses
1 egg
2 cups flour

¼ teaspoon salt
2 teaspoons baking soda
1 teaspoon each, cinnamon,
  cloves and ginger
sugar for rolling

PLAY-BY-PLAY

1. Preheat oven to 350 degrees.

2. Cream shortening and sugar. Add molasses and egg. Stir in remaining ingredients.

3. Shape dough into small balls, then roll in additional sugar. Arrange on cookie sheets and bake for 8 minutes.

Makes 2½ dozen cookies

If you like moister cookies, underbake 1 minute.

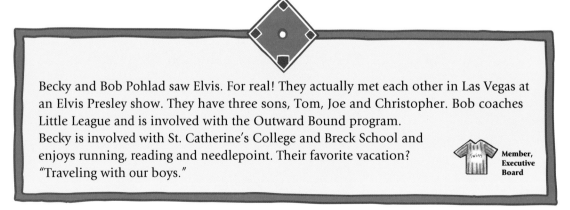

Becky and Bob Pohlad saw Elvis. For real! They actually met each other in Las Vegas at an Elvis Presley show. They have three sons, Tom, Joe and Christopher. Bob coaches Little League and is involved with the Outward Bound program.
Becky is involved with St. Catherine's College and Breck School and enjoys running, reading and needlepoint. Their favorite vacation? "Traveling with our boys."

Member, Executive Board

Next-Best-Thing To Robert Redford

from Robin and Lenny Webster

LINE UP

1 cup flour
½ cup butter, softened
1 cup finely chopped pecans
8 ounces cream cheese, softened
1 cup sugar
12 ounces Cool Whip, thawed

1 3.4-ounce package vanilla
  pudding mix
1 3.9-ounce package chocolate
  pudding mix
3 cups milk

PLAY-BY-PLAY

1. Preheat oven to 350 degrees.

2. Combine flour, butter and pecans until crumb-like. Press into 9-by-13-inch baking pan. Bake for 15-20 minutes. Cool.

3. Beat cream cheese and sugar. Fold in half of Cool Whip and spread over crust.

4. Combine pudding mixes and beat in milk. Spread over cream cheese layer. Top pudding layer with remaining Cool Whip. Cover and refrigerate overnight.

Serves 8-10

Line Drive Lemon Bars

from Cori and Pat Meares

" This recipe originated from my maternal grandmother. I now bake these bars for my two most important men—my father, Ernie, and my husband, Pat. "

—Cori Meares

LINE UP

1 cup margarine, softened
1½ cups flour
½ cup powdered sugar,
   plus more for top
3 eggs, beaten

1 cup sugar
3 tablespoons lemon juice
1 tablespoon lemon zest
   (see page 128)
pinch salt

PLAY-BY-PLAY

1. Preheat oven to 350 degrees.

2. Mix margarine, flour and powdered sugar until crumbly. Press into 9-by-13-inch baking pan. Bake for 20 minutes.

3. Meanwhile, combine remaining ingredients, mixing well. Pour over baked crust. Bake for 20 minutes longer. Cool and sift additional powdered sugar over top and cut into squares.

Serves 12

No-Bake Cookies

from Lori and Jim Deshaies

LINE UP

2 cups sugar
¼ cup cocoa
dash salt
½ cup milk

½ cup margarine
½ cup smooth peanut butter
3 cups oatmeal
2 teaspoons vanilla

PLAY-BY-PLAY

1. In large saucepan, bring sugar, cocoa, salt, milk and margarine to full boil for 1 minute. Remove from heat.

2. Stir in peanut butter and blend well. Add oatmeal and vanilla. Drop by spoonfuls onto waxed paper. Cool and eat.

Makes 4 dozen cookies

❝ Don't make these when you're alone, they're much too easy to make and eat. ❞

—Lori Deshaies

Jim, Lori, Molly, and Libby

Minne-Soda (Twins) Cracker Cookies

from Jana and Jeff Reboulet

LINE UP

40 squares saltine crackers
1 cup margarine

1 cup brown sugar
12 ounces chocolate chips, melted

Jeff, Jana, and Jason

PLAY-BY-PLAY

1. Preheat oven to 400 degrees. Line baking sheet or jelly roll pan with foil. Position crackers close together on foil.

2. Boil margarine and brown sugar for 3 minutes. Pour over crackers and bake for 5-6 minutes.

3. Spread chocolate over all. Place in freezer or refrigerator until chocolate is set. Break into pieces. Store in a plastic bag or airtight container, keep cool.

Makes 2½ dozen treats

Apple Crisp

from Monica and Bill Mahre

LINE UP

1 cup flour
1 cup brown sugar
1 cup oatmeal
½ cup butter, softened

4 cups apples, peeled and cored
½ cup sugar
1 tablespoon cinnamon

PLAY-BY-PLAY

1. Preheat oven to 350 degrees. Grease 9-by-13-inch baking pan.

2. Combine flour, brown sugar, oatmeal and softened butter for topping. Set aside.

3. Slice apples into baking pan and sprinkle with sugar and cinnamon. Spread topping over apples and bake 30 minutes, until apples are tender and bubbly.

Serves 12

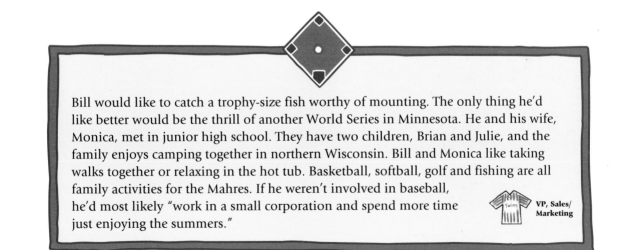

Bill would like to catch a trophy-size fish worthy of mounting. The only thing he'd like better would be the thrill of another World Series in Minnesota. He and his wife, Monica, met in junior high school. They have two children, Brian and Julie, and the family enjoys camping together in northern Wisconsin. Bill and Monica like taking walks together or relaxing in the hot tub. Basketball, softball, golf and fishing are all family activities for the Mahres. If he weren't involved in baseball, he'd most likely "work in a small corporation and spend more time just enjoying the summers."

VP, Sales/ Marketing

Caught Stealing Banana Pudding

from Robin and Lenny Webster

ff This pudding is one of our favorite desserts that we have at Thanksgiving and Christmas. *ff*

—Robin Webster

LINE UP

1 5.1-ounce box instant vanilla
　pudding
8 ounces sour cream

12 ounces Cool Whip, thawed
1 12-ounce box of vanilla wafers
5 ripe bananas, sliced

PLAY-BY-PLAY

1. Prepare pudding as directed on package. Fold in sour cream and Cool Whip.

2. Line a large serving dish with a layer of vanilla wafers. Top with half the banana slices. Cover with half the pudding. Repeat layers ending with a sprinkling of crushed vanilla wafers.

3. Chill for at least 1 hour before serving.

Serves 16-20

Use a 4-quart oblong dish.

Bases Loaded Banana Split Pie

from Diane and Dick Martin

LINE UP

2 cups crumbled vanilla wafers
½ cup butter, melted
½ cup butter, softened
8 ounces cream cheese, softened
2 cups powdered sugar
2 bananas, sliced

1 20-ounce can crushed
   pineapple, drained
12 ounces Cool Whip, thawed
maraschino cherries and chopped
   nuts, as desired

PLAY-BY-PLAY

1. Combine vanilla wafer crumbs and melted butter. Press into 9-by-13-inch baking pan.

2. Cream softened butter, cream cheese and sugar. Spread over crust. Layer bananas and pineapple over cream cheese mixture. Top with Cool Whip. Sprinkle with cherries and nuts, as desired.

Serves 6-8

Bill's Blueberry Dessert

from Monica and Bill Mahre

❝ This dessert is my favorite. The recipe has been handed down in my family. ❞

—Monica Mahre

LINE UP

20 graham crackers, crushed
¼ cup melted butter
¾ cup sugar, divided
2 eggs
8 ounces cream cheese, softened

½ teaspoon vanilla
¼ teaspoon salt
1 21-ounce can blueberry
    pie filling
whipped cream or ice cream

PLAY-BY-PLAY

1. Preheat oven to 375 degrees.

2. Combine crushed graham crackers, melted butter and ¼ cup sugar. Pat into bottom of 9-by-13-inch baking pan.

3. Beat eggs. Add cream cheese, ½ cup sugar, vanilla and salt. Mix until smooth. Pour over crust. Bake for 15-20 minutes. Allow to cool.

4. Spread blueberry filling over dessert and refrigerate at least 1 hour. Serve with whipped cream or ice cream.

Serves 12-15

Top of the Order Blueberry Tart

from Andrea and Mark Guthrie

Mark, Andrea, and Kevin, with Scott Erickson

LINE UP

½ cup plus 2 tablespoons butter,
   softened
1⅓ cups flour
¼ teaspoon salt
3 cups fresh blueberries

¾ cup sugar
3 tablespoons cornstarch
⅔ cup water
1½ teaspoons lemon juice

PLAY-BY-PLAY

1. Preheat oven to 375 degrees.

2. Combine ½ cup of the butter, flour and salt until well blended and dough sticks together when pressed. If too dry, add 1 tablespoon milk. Press into bottom and up sides of 10-inch tart pan. Bake for 15 minutes and let cool.

3. Combine 1 cup of the blueberries, sugar, cornstarch and water in large saucepan. Cook over medium low heat until thick. Remove from heat, cool slightly.

4. Add remaining 2 tablespoons butter, 2 cups blueberries and lemon juice to filling. Pour into tart shell and refrigerate until served.

Serves 8-10

Hall of Fame Holiday Bread Pudding

from Nita and Harmon Killebrew

Holidays are happy and active at the Killebrew home, where they have a traditional "Holiday Gong Show." "The most popular act so far has been Harmon's performance as 'Moxy Marilyn,' where he sings 'Happy Birthday, Mr. President' while sitting on someone's lap," says Nita.

LINE UP

5 cups bread cubes and crumbs
2½ cups warm milk
¾ cup butter, softened
½ cup sugar
1 tablespoon cinnamon
1 teaspoon nutmeg

2 tablespoons plus 1 teaspoon
 vanilla
4 eggs, beaten
1 cup raisins
⅓ cup chopped walnuts
2 cups powdered sugar

PLAY-BY-PLAY

1. Preheat oven to 350 degrees. Grease 2-quart casserole.

2. Combine bread and milk in casserole.

3. Cream ¼ cup of the butter and sugar. Add cinnamon, nutmeg, 1 teaspoon of the vanilla and eggs. Pour over bread-milk mixture and stir gently. Stir in raisins and nuts.

4. Bake for 50-60 minutes, until pudding is set. When done, a butter knife inserted in center should come out clean.

5. Meanwhile, combine powdered sugar, ½ cup butter, 1 tablespoon water and remaining 2 tablespoons vanilla in a small bowl. Beat with mixer at high speed until well blended. Cover and refrigerate until serving over warm pudding.

Serves 10

Aunt Helen's Cheese Torte

from Karilyn and Terry Ryan

LINE UP

2 cups graham cracker crumbs
½ cup melted butter
1½ cups sugar
dash cinnamon
1 3-ounce box lemon jello

1 cup boiling water
8 ounces cream cheese
2 teaspoons vanilla
1 pint whipping cream
fruit topping, if desired

PLAY-BY-PLAY

1. Preheat oven to 350 degrees.

2. Combine graham cracker crumbs, melted butter, ½ cup of the sugar and a dash of cinnamon. Reserve ¼ cup for topping. Pat remaining mixture into 8-by-12-inch baking pan. Bake for 10 minutes.

3. Dissolve jello in boiling water. Cool. Cream together cream cheese, remaining 1 cup sugar, and vanilla. Beat whipping cream into cream cheese mixture until stiff.

4. Fold cooled jello into whipped cream cheese and cream mixture. Pour over crust. Sprinkle with reserved crumb mixture. Chill. Serve with fruit topping.

Serves 10

Seventh Inning Slice

from Donna and Greg Brummett

LINE UP

1 cup butter or margarine,
    softened
1¾ cup sugar
4 eggs
1 teaspoon vanilla
2½ cups flour

1½ teaspoons baking powder
pinch salt
2 21-ounce cans cherry pie
    filling
¾ cup powdered sugar
2 tablespoons milk

PLAY-BY-PLAY

1. Preheat oven to 350 degrees. Grease a jelly roll pan.

2. Beat butter, sugar, eggs, and vanilla until well blended.
Add flour, baking powder and salt. Reserve 1½ cups batter.
Spread remaining batter into pan.

3. Top with cherry filling. Drop remaining batter by spoonfuls
over filling. Bake for 35-40 minutes. Let cool.

4. Combine powdered sugar and milk. Drizzle over bars.

Serves 10-12

"My wife Donna and I love the same foods — home-cooked meals. I always try to eat
a big pasta meal on the day I pitch. Lasagna is my favorite," says Greg. The Brummetts
make their off-season home in Wichita, Kansas, but like most baseball families, they
move around a lot. They like the shopping and restaurants in Dallas, the holiday lights
on The Plaza in Kansas City, the Mall of America and anywhere they can go fishing.
Greg also enjoys hunting and playing golf. Donna loves to read, walk and cross-stitch.
Both the Brummetts like country music. The Brummetts will be
opening the 1994 season with an expanded family roster; their first
child is due in April.

57 **Pitcher**

Chocolate Mint Silk Pie

from Rosemary and Brett Merriman

Rosemary, Brett, and Alec Trey

LINE UP

1½ cups crushed Oreo cookies
½ cup melted butter
1 cup sugar
¾ cup butter or margarine, softened
3 ounces semisweet chocolate, melted and cooled
½ teaspoon peppermint extract
3 eggs
sweetened whipped cream

PLAY-BY-PLAY

1. Combine crushed Oreos and melted butter and press into bottom and sides of 9-inch pie plate. Refrigerate for 10 minutes.

2. Cream sugar and softened butter. Add chocolate and peppermint extract, continuing beating for 2 minutes. Add eggs and continue beating, scraping bowl often, until light and fluffy, about 5 minutes.

3. Spoon mixture into crust and refrigerate for 3 hours. Serve with whipped cream.

Serves 10

Big Train Chocolate Pecan Clusters

from Rachel and Carl Willis

LINE UP

1 7-ounce jar marshmallow
    creme
1½ pounds chocolate kisses,
    foil removed

5 cups sugar
1 13-ounce can evaporated milk
½ cup butter
6 cups pecans, broken into pieces

PLAY-BY-PLAY

1. Place marshmallow creme and chocolate kisses in large bowl and set aside.

2. Combine sugar, evaporated milk and butter in saucepan and bring to boil. Cook for 8 minutes, stirring often.

3. Pour over marshmallow creme and chocolate kisses and blend well. Stir in pecans and quickly drop by spoonfuls onto waxed paper. Candy will thicken as it cools, so work as quickly as you can.

Makes 3 dozen clusters

Sharon, Kevin,
and Sarah

Dirt in a Pail

from Sharon and Kevin Tapani

LINE UP

2 cups cold milk
1 3.9-ounce box instant
    chocolate pudding
14 Oreo cookies, crushed

1½ cups Cool Whip, thawed
small plastic pail
gummy worms and candy flowers

❝ Our daughter
loves to play in
the mud. She
thinks 'eating
dirt' for dessert
is great fun. ❞

—Sharon Tapani

PLAY-BY-PLAY

1. Pour milk into pail or bowl. Add pudding and whisk.
Let stand until slightly thickened.

2. Stir 1 cup of the crushed cookies and Cool Whip into pudding.
Top with remaining cookies. Decorate with gummy worms or
candy flowers.

Makes 1 pail of fun for kids

207

Full Count Flan

from Gordette and Tony Oliva

LINE UP

1 14-ounce can sweetened
    condensed milk
1 12-ounce can evaporated
    whole milk
4 eggs, slightly beaten with fork

½ teaspoon salt
1 teaspoon vanilla
¾ cup sugar
1 tablespoon water

PLAY-BY-PLAY

1. Preheat oven to 350 degrees.

2. Combine milks, eggs, salt and vanilla. Set aside.

3. Combine sugar and water over medium-high heat, stirring constantly until dark golden. Immediately swirl in bottom and sides of 8-inch mold. Pour flan mixture over caramel.

4. Place mold in larger pan of water. Water should not be more than half-way up the side of the mold.

5. Bake for 45-60 minutes. When flan is set, quickly unmold onto serving dish. Serve warm.

Serves 6

Mom's Fruit-filled Tart

from Danielle and Derek Parks

LINE UP

1 egg
1 cup plain yogurt
½ cup plus 1 tablespoon
    margarine
1 cup sugar

3 cups flour
1 teaspoon baking powder
1 21-ounce can fruit pie filling,
    or 2 cups fresh fruit
1 egg white, beaten
cinnamon

PLAY-BY-PLAY

1. Preheat oven to 325 degrees.

2. Mix together all ingredients except fruit, egg white and cinnamon. Blend well, then divide in half. Roll out half of dough and fit to bottom of 10-inch tart pan. Top with fruit filling.

3. Roll out remaining dough and cut into strips with pastry wheel or sharp knife. Arrange strips over filling to form lattice. Brush with egg white and sprinkle with cinnamon.

4. Bake for 35-40 minutes, until crust is golden and fruit bubbles.

Serves 8

❝ Derek and my little brother Doug played Pony League baseball together. In fact, I can remember sitting at a Pony League game commenting to my mom, 'Hey that Derek Parks kid is good looking, too bad he's in eighth grade' (At the time I was a junior in high school— UGH!). ❞

—Danielle Parks

209

Oreo Cookie Freeze

from Rachel and Carl Willis

❝ This recipe was handed down from Carl's mom, Ola Willis. ❞

—Rachael Willis

LINE UP

28 Oreo cookies, crushed
¼ cup melted butter
½ gallon Oreo, vanilla, or
    chocolate chip ice cream,
    softened
1 cup sugar
1 12-ounce can evaporated milk

1 teaspoon vanilla
4 ounces semi-sweet chocolate,
    melted
¼ cup plus 2 tablespoons butter
1 cup chopped pecans
16 ounces Cool Whip, thawed

PLAY-BY-PLAY

1. Mix Oreos with melted butter. Press firmly into the bottom of 9-by-13-inch baking pan and freeze 30 minutes.

2. Spread softened ice cream over frozen cookie crust. Beating soft ice cream with an electric mixer makes it easy to spread. Return dessert to freezer for 30 minutes.

3. Meanwhile, combine sugar, milk, vanilla, melted chocolate and ¼ cup plus 2 tablespoons butter in saucepan. Boil 1 minute. Let cool, then spread over frozen ice cream and return to freezer.

4. Mix pecans into Cool Whip and spread over chocolate. Store in freezer.

Serves 8-10

Simple Peach Cobbler

from Lisa Limbaugh and Eddie Guardado

LINE UP

½ cup butter
1 cup self-rising flour
1 cup sugar

1 cup sliced peaches
1 cup milk

PLAY-BY-PLAY

1. Preheat oven to 350 degrees. Melt butter in 9-inch square baking pan.

2. Add flour, sugar, peaches and milk to butter—do not mix!

3. Bake for 50 minutes, or until golden. Serve hot with ice cream.

Serves 8-10

Peaches and Cream Kuchen

from Nancy and John Gordon

John and Nancy Gordon met at a Halloween party. "She told me to take my mask off and I didn't have one on," he jokes.

LINE UP

2 cups flour
¾ cup sugar
½ teaspoon salt
¼ teaspoon baking powder
½ cup margarine

1 30-ounce can peach halves
   or slices
1 teaspoon cinnamon
2 egg yolks
1 cup heavy cream

PLAY-BY-PLAY

1. Preheat oven to 400 degrees.

2. Combine flour, 2 tablespoons of the sugar, salt and baking powder. Cut in margarine with pastry blender or two knives until mixture is crumbly.

3. Pat dough firmly against bottom and sides of 8-inch square baking pan. Arrange peaches over crust. Combine remaining sugar and cinnamon, sprinkle over peaches. Bake for 15 minutes.

4. Beat egg yolks with cream. Pour over peaches. Bake for 30 minutes longer, until golden. Serve warm or chilled.

Serves 6

A pastry blender is a handle fitted with loops of wire or dull blades, used to "cut" butter into dry ingredients. If you don't have one, use a fork, two knives held together, or your fingers.

Pat's Peanut Butter Cups

from Cori and Pat Meares

LINE UP

1 cup melted margarine
1 pound powdered sugar
1 cup peanut butter

⅓ of a 1-pound box graham
    crackers, crushed
12 ounces chocolate chips

PLAY-BY-PLAY

1. Grease 9-by-13-inch baking pan.

2. Combine margarine, powdered sugar, peanut butter and crushed graham crackers. Press firmly into pan.

3. Melt chocolate chips and pour over candy. Immediately cut into little squares. Refrigerate. After chocolate sets and candy is hard, cut again.

Serves 10

Place crackers in a self-sealing plastic bag and roll over with a rolling pin to crush.

❝ It's amazing that it's a tradition in *both* my family and my wife Cori's family to have turkey, dressing, mashed potatoes, gravy, green bean casserole, rolls, a relish tray, broccoli and rice casserole and homemade pies for Thanksgiving *and* Christmas dinners. **❞**

—Pat Meares

Jorgy's Pistachio Torte

from Sue and Terry Jorgensen

❝ Terry's favorite dessert. ❞

—Sue Jorgensen

LINE UP

½ cup butter, softened
2 teaspoons sugar
1 cup flour
¼ cup chopped walnuts or
    pecans
8 ounces cream cheese, softened
1 cup powdered sugar

16 ounces Cool Whip, thawed
2 3.4-ounce packages instant
    pistachio pudding
2½ cups milk
chopped walnuts or pecans
cherries

PLAY-BY-PLAY

1. Preheat oven to 375 degrees.

2. Cream butter with sugar until light. Add flour and ¼ cup nuts. Pat into 9-by-13-inch baking pan. Bake for 15 minutes. Cool.

3. Beat together cream cheese, powdered sugar and Cool Whip. Pour half over cooled crust.

4. Blend pudding mix with milk. Spread over cream cheese layer. Cover pudding with remaining cream cheese mixture. Sprinkle with chopped nuts and cherries for garnish.

Serves 8

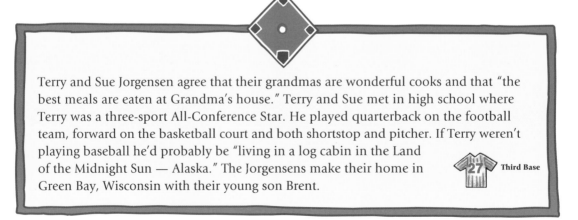

Terry and Sue Jorgensen agree that their grandmas are wonderful cooks and that "the best meals are eaten at Grandma's house." Terry and Sue met in high school where Terry was a three-sport All-Conference Star. He played quarterback on the football team, forward on the basketball court and both shortstop and pitcher. If Terry weren't playing baseball he'd probably be "living in a log cabin in the Land of the Midnight Sun — Alaska." The Jorgensens make their home in Green Bay, Wisconsin with their young son Brent.

27 Third Base

Bourbon Street Praline Candy

from Tonya and Dave Winfield

LINE UP

2 cups evaporated milk
¼ cup butter

2 cups sugar
1½ cups pecan pieces

PLAY-BY-PLAY

1. Butter a 20-inch long piece of waxed paper. The candy will be placed here to cool and harden.

2. Combine milk, butter and sugar in sauce pan over medium-low heat. Stir mixture constantly until it thickens, about 15-20 minutes. If using a double boiler, it is not necessary to stir constantly.

3. Have ready a glass of cold water to test the candy. Once the mixture has thickened, put a few drops into the water. Roll between your fingers to see if drops form a soft ball. Test the candy this way, using a fresh glass of cold water, until it forms a soft ball.

4. When candy comes to correct consistency, add pecans and mix well. Turn off heat. Drop candy by spoonfuls onto buttered waxed paper. Let stand to cool and harden.

Makes 12-16 pralines

❝ This recipe has been in my family for over 40 years. It is wonderful anytime of year, especially the holidays. ❞

—Tonya Winfield

Kitty's Ricotta Puffs

from Mary Ann and Jim Kaat

The Kaat family *loves* Italian food. "It has always been a family tradition to eat Italian dinners together," says Jim. "My wife Mary Ann and I, along with our four grown children, now get together at our home in Stuart, Florida for these family feasts."

LINE UP

3 eggs
4 teaspoons baking powder
2 tablespoons sugar
1 pound ricotta cheese

¼ teaspoon salt
1 cup flour
hot oil for deep frying
powdered sugar for rolling

PLAY-BY-PLAY

1. Beat eggs until fluffy. Add baking powder, sugar and ricotta, mix well. Add salt and flour and mix thoroughly.

2. In deep fryer or pan, heat 3 inches of oil to 375 degrees.

3. Drop batter by teaspoonful into hot oil and fry for 2-3 minutes, turning often, until golden.

4. With slotted spoon, remove puffs to paper towels to drain. Roll in powdered sugar if desired.

Makes 40 puffs

Rhubarb Custard Meringue Pie

from Eloise and Carl Pohlad

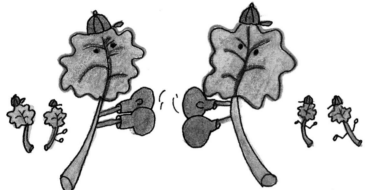

LINE UP

3 cups chopped rhubarb
1¾ cups plus 2 tablespoons sugar
2 rounded tablespoons flour
3 eggs, separated
½ cup milk

2 tablespoons melted butter
1 tablespoon lemon juice
1 unbaked 9-inch pie crust
¼ teaspoon cream of tartar
½ teaspoon vanilla

PLAY-BY-PLAY

1. Preheat oven to 425 degrees.

2. Combine rhubarb, 1½ cups of the sugar, flour, egg yolks, milk, butter and lemon juice. Pour into pie shell and bake 40-45 minutes. Remove from oven and turn oven down to 400 degrees.

3. Beat egg whites with cream of tartar at medium speed until soft peaks form. Increase speed to high and gradually add remaining ¼ cup plus 2 tablespoons sugar and vanilla. Beat until stiff.

4. Spoon meringue over pie, making sure to seal to crust. Bake for 8-10 minutes, until lightly golden.

Serves 6-8

Strawberry Banana Pie

from Pedro Muñoz

LINE UP

2 pints strawberries, hulled
   and sliced
2 large bananas, sliced thin

½ cup strawberry glaze
1 9-inch pie shell, baked
1 cup whipped cream

PLAY-BY-PLAY

1. Combine fruits and strawberry glaze in bowl. Mix well.

2. Spoon mixture into pie shell. Refrigerate at least 2 hours. Garnish with whipped cream and serve.

Serves 8

Triple Play Trifle

from Jeanie and Kent Hrbek

LINE UP

1 custard angel food cake,
    ripped into small chunks
¼ cup plus 2 tablespoons
    brandy, if desired
3 cups vanilla custard or
    pudding, made with half
    and half instead of milk

1 pound each: blueberries,
    raspberries and strawberries,
    drained if frozen, or
    measure 2 cups each if fresh
3 cups heavy cream, whipped

PLAY-BY-PLAY

1. Use your largest glass serving bowl or a trifle bowl (a tall, clear glass, straight-sided serving bowl on a pedestal). Scatter one third of the cake over bottom of bowl. Drizzle with 2 tablespoons brandy, if desired.

2. Over cake, layer one third each of the custard, fruit and whipped cream. Repeat two more times beginning with cake and brandy, and ending with whipped cream.

Serves 12

Wedding Reception Kiss, 1985

WHO'S WHO

22

23

24

See page 239

Index

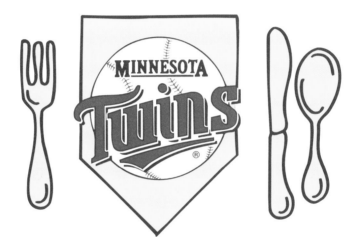

WHO'S WHO ANSWERS

Notes

Notes

Notes

Notes

Notes

Notes